Instant Debian – Build a Web Server

Build strong foundations for your future-ready web application using the universal operating system, Debian

Jose Miguel Parrella

BIRMINGHAM - MUMBAI

Instant Debian – Build a Web Server

First published: September 2013

Production Reference: 1230913

Published by Packt Publishing Ltd.
Livery Place
35 Livery Street
Birmingham B3 2PB, UK.

ISBN 978-1-84951-884-0

www.packtpub.com

Credits

Author
Jose Miguel Parrella

Reviewer
Gunnar Wolf

Acquisition Editor
Andrew Duckworth

Commissioning Editor
Neil Alexander

Technical Editor
Kanhucharan Panda

Adrian Raposo

Copy Editor
Gladson Monteiro

Kirti Pai

Project Coordinator
Amigya Khurana

Proofreader
Bridget Braund

Production Coordinator
Pooja Chiplunkar

Cover Work
Pooja Chiplunkar

Cover Image
Yuvraj Mannari

About the Author

Jose Miguel Parrella has been involved in the world of open source since he was 14, during his freshman year at college. In Venezuela, he's worked for the Intellectual Property Office, the National Electric Corporation, and other government entities, leading several Linux-based projects.

He was the CTO of an open source consulting firm in Venezuela and Ecuador, helping to grow the business and developing a strong team that delivered dozens of successful Linux projects, including the architecture, development, and release of Canaima National GNU/Linux 2.0 distribution of Venezuela used in over two million netbooks. He is currently on an assignment as an open source Specialist for a large IT company in the United States.

Since 2005, Jose Miguel has been involved in the Debian Project, speaking at several DebConfs, and became a Debian Developer in 2007. He uploaded Nginx 0.4 on the Debian archive in 2006.

In addition to workshops and keynotes delivered across the globe and publications, such as the Rapid Distribution Deployment whitepaper, Jose Miguel has been a technical reviewer for two Packt Publishing books on Nginx and is currently working on other titles related to open source software.

His opinions in this book or elsewhere don't necessarily represent the views of his past or present employers and/or the Debian Project.

I would like to thank my wife, Ailé, for her leadership, professionalism, and support in my life. You rock! And I would also like to thank all the Debian Project volunteers for their hard and high-quality work, as well as the managers and partners who have provided me with learning opportunities in the past. Thank you all.

About the Reviewer

Gunnar Wolf has been a Free Software enthusiast and promoter for over 15 years, choosing GNU/Linux for his production servers as early as 1996. Computer administration and security has always been one of his main topics of interest and research.

In the early 2000s, he founded the National Conference on Free Software (CONSOL), which helped consolidate the Mexican Free Software communities, and led its work for several years. In 2003, he became a Debian Developer and has been an organizer for the yearly Debian Conference since 2005.

In 2005, he started working at the Economics Research Institute of the National Autonomous University of Mexico (IIEc-UNAM) as a systems and network administrator, and a Web applications programmer. All of the systems he administers run Debian. He teaches the course on Operating Systems at the Engineering Faculty of the same university.

He has taken the topic of Free Software as a personal passion, as a particular expression of a much wider movement, Free Culture. He has also participated as a coordinator and co-author for the book *Construcción Colaborativa del Conocimiento* (IIEc-UNAM, 2011).

His recent thoughts and experiences in life are often portrayed in his personal blog, `http://gwolf.org/`.

www.PacktPub.com

Support files, eBooks, discount offers and more

You might want to visit www.PacktPub.com for support files and downloads related to your book.

Did you know that Packt offers eBook versions of every book published, with PDF and ePub files available? You can upgrade to the eBook version at www.PacktPub.com and as a print book customer, you are entitled to a discount on the eBook copy. Get in touch with us at service@packtpub.com for more details.

At www.PacktPub.com, you can also read a collection of free technical articles, sign up for a range of free newsletters and receive exclusive discounts and offers on Packt books and eBooks.

http://PacktLib.PacktPub.com

Do you need instant solutions to your IT questions? PacktLib is Packt's online digital book library. Here, you can access, read and search across Packt's entire library of books.

Why Subscribe?

- Fully searchable across every book published by Packt
- Copy and paste, print and bookmark content
- On demand and accessible via web browser

Free Access for Packt account holders

If you have an account with Packt at www.PacktPub.com, you can use this to access PacktLib today and view nine entirely free books. Simply use your login credentials for immediate access.

Table of Contents

Preface

APT, one of the technologies that made Debian (and its derivatives, such as Ubuntu) highly popular, became mainstream for production deployments during the same time span that web applications broke through the barriers of enterprise fitness, reliability, and scalability.

The flexibility of Debian systems makes it very appealing for web DevOps and modern web apps. This book tries to simplify deployment and reduce time-to-market, while providing a solid foundation for you to grow your Debian sysadmin practices.

What this book covers

In the first part of the book we'll help you choose the right flavor of Debian, install it, and prepare for multiple and massive installations, should you need it. We will also guide you through the initial APT setup, installing the stack, and configuring storage and frameworks.

In the second part of the book, we harden the installation, analyze scalability paths, and learn how to effectively maintain your system, including backup/restore and performance. We also provide a future look at cloud and incident response, which will help you get the most out of your installation in the long run.

Choosing the right flavor of Debian (Simple) explains how Debian organizes software, the architectures, and installation methods, and indicates a set of criteria for system administrators to choose and get the right media.

Installing Debian GNU/Linux (Simple) goes through the installation process, including partitioning, networking, and using tasksel to install an initial set of packages to work with.

Making Debian GNU/Linux installations scalable (Medium) discusses methods to automate and scale Debian installations, such as debconf preseeding.

Preparing the APT packaging system for your environment (Simple) explains how to configure APT and use APT tools, such as apt-get for package management.

Installing your application platform stack (Simple) goes through the installation of an Apache or Nginx stack, as well as PHP and other components, and the databases—all in the Debian way.

Setting up your storage, security, and permissions (Simple) goes through the mount-level and user-level options to implement a security strategy for your application storage.

Setting up your database/data storage (Medium) explores how to configure the databases and their underlying storage.

Configuring your programming language libraries (Medium) discusses the Debian way to install a framework or a set of libraries, where it adds value, and where it needs administering.

Setting up secure remote support options (Simple) goes through the simple but necessary changes, necessary on a Debian system, in order to facilitate a more secure working environment.

Keeping your system up-to-date (Simple) teaches us that with thousands of developers maintaining the most exciting open source projects, it's important to know how to and when to install updates on Debian.

Backing up your environment (Medium) describes a backup and restore strategy from an outcome-oriented vision using simple tools and dedicated backup software.

Restoring your environment (Simple) discusses the scenarios where fast restoring of data is critical to the application.

Preparing for common security scenarios (Medium) tackles several of the most common security scenarios and how to move from reactive to proactive security.

Reading logs and troubleshooting your setup (Simple) goes through the most important logfiles and essential skills to troubleshoot, by interpreting them.

Using proxies, caches, and clusters to scale your architecture (Advanced) discusses architectural scenarios for future growth of the application, including proxies, caches, and clusters, and when they can add value.

Consuming Windows Azure Cloud Services (Medium) provides a specific example of how to consume public cloud services for extending the application.

Responding to security incidents (Advanced) discusses several steps and outcomes in the face of a security incident.

Monitoring your server's operation (Medium) goes through several of the most common data points for a web-based application, and how to collect, compare, and process them.

Optimizing your solution performance (Advanced) discusses not only the low-hanging fruit for web application performance improvement, but also the potentially bigger improvements of fundamental debugging and optimization.

What you need for this book

You need hardware, either a server or hypervisor software that supports Linux-based operating systems to install Debian. You should plan for at least 2 GB of disk space, and additional space for your database and application, including static files. You also need a broadband Internet connection to download the installation media as well as any additional software packages.

Who this book is for

Readers should be familiar with the essential concepts of the Linux system's administration, such as how to work with files and permissions, command line instructions, and how service and processes work in Linux, although the chapters are not technically demanding. While the book does not require previous knowledge on the APT system, it does expect readers to understand how the particular configuration files for the services Apache, Nginx, MySQL, PostgreSQL, and so on, work.

Conventions

In this book, you will find a number of styles of text that distinguish between different kinds of information. Here are some examples of these styles, and an explanation of their meaning.

Code words in text are shown as follows: "You can always delete those partitions and give space back to /var and /tmp."

A block of code is set as follows:

```php
<?php
  $mc = new Memcached();
  $mc->addServer("localhost", 11211);
  $value = file_get_contents('/var/www/icon.jpg');
  $mc->set("/icon.jpg", $value);
?>
```

Any command-line input or output is written as follows:

```
chown -R www-data:www-data /var/www # resets owner and group to www-data
```

New terms and **important words** are shown in bold. Words that you see on the screen, in menus or dialog boxes for example, appear in the text like this: ". You might choose **Graphical Install**, which will run you through the same prompts but with mouse support, colors, buttons and scrollbars.".

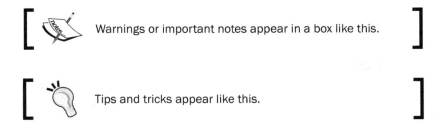

Warnings or important notes appear in a box like this.

Tips and tricks appear like this.

Reader feedback

Feedback from our readers is always welcome. Let us know what you think about this book—what you liked or may have disliked. Reader feedback is important for us to develop titles that you really get the most out of.

To send us general feedback, simply send an e-mail to feedback@packtpub.com, and mention the book title via the subject of your message.

If there is a topic that you have expertise in and you are interested in either writing or contributing to a book, see our author guide on www.packtpub.com/authors.

Customer support

Now that you are the proud owner of a Packt book, we have a number of things to help you to get the most from your purchase.

Downloading the example code

You can download the example code files for all Packt books you have purchased from your account at http://www.packtpub.com. If you purchased this book elsewhere, you can visit http://www.packtpub.com/support and register to have the files e-mailed directly to you.

Errata

Although we have taken every care to ensure the accuracy of our content, mistakes do happen. If you find a mistake in one of our books—maybe a mistake in the text or the code—we would be grateful if you would report this to us. By doing so, you can save other readers from frustration and help us improve subsequent versions of this book. If you find any errata, please report them by visiting http://www.packtpub.com/submit-errata, selecting your book, clicking on the **errata submission form** link, and entering the details of your errata. Once your errata are verified, your submission will be accepted and the errata will be uploaded on our website, or added to any list of existing errata, under the Errata section of that title. Any existing errata can be viewed by selecting your title from http://www.packtpub.com/support.

Piracy

Piracy of copyright material on the Internet is an ongoing problem across all media. At Packt, we take the protection of our copyright and licenses very seriously. If you come across any illegal copies of our works, in any form, on the Internet, please provide us with the location address or website name immediately so that we can pursue a remedy.

Please contact us at copyright@packtpub.com with a link to the suspected pirated material.

We appreciate your help in protecting our authors, and our ability to bring you valuable content.

Questions

You can contact us at questions@packtpub.com if you are having a problem with any aspect of the book, and we will do our best to address it.

Debian – Build a Web Server

Welcome to *Instant Debian – Build a Web Server*.

With the advent of social computing and the explosion of data and API-based economies, web applications are taken to a whole new level. They are not the vehicle but the center of gravity of a big part of the IT industry, including the enterprise customers.

No longer do companies choose a technology stack just because of features but because of reduced time to market, which enables them to grow faster and accommodate demand while keeping a sane bottom line.

Debian has a long-standing tradition as a very flexible GNU/Linux-based distribution, in part because of its packaging system and also because it has been made possible by a dynamic community of developers and maintainers.

Even though it is a proven platform for web applications, most web developers face steep learning curves. Maybe this happens because they are not familiar with GNU/Linux, they have an enterprise experience with other packaging systems such as RPM, or because they traditionally didn't manage aspects such as performance or security.

Although it's meant to be just a starting point in your Debian journey, the standardized instructions in this book, such as using `sudo` or `apt-get`, can be replicated across most administrative and development scenarios you will encounter in the future.

The book also outlines an effective approach to performance and scaling by presenting different architectures that can help accommodate growth, including cloud computing, where Debian can run as a workload to increase your efficiencies.

This micro book covers the decision-making process, installation, and configuration of a solid foundation on which you can deploy web-based applications on Debian—whether they are written on PHP, Perl, Python, or Ruby.

Starting off by providing a little knowledge of Debian, this book will guide you to a properly configured system that tackles the most common pitfalls DevOps encounter, such as partitioning, filesystem permissions, or scaling, thereby providing a straightforward approach to Debian for web applications.

Without further ado, we can proceed to the first set of recipes.

Choosing the right flavor of Debian (Simple)

The Debian Project prides itself on producing the Universal Operating System. This means that the software the project puts together runs on a broad set of hardware (architectures) for several types of purposes, and even for different kernels such as Linux, Hurd, or FreeBSD.

Choosing the right flavor of Debian for your setup might seem intimidating at first, but this recipe will provide you with decision elements to help you reduce your time to market with Debian and choose the right architecture and installation method, particularly for a web server.

Getting ready

At any point in time, Debian has three different branches available for use: stable, testing, and unstable. Think of unstable as the cutting edge of free software; it has reasonably modern software packages, and sometimes those packages introduce changes or features that may break the user experience. After an amount of time has passed (usually 10 days, but it depends on the package's upload priority), the new software is considered to be relatively safe to use and is moved to testing. Testing can provide a good balance between modern software and relatively reliable software. Testing goes through several iterations during the course of several years, and eventually it's frozen for a new stable release. This stable release is supported by the Debian Project for a number of years, including feature and security updates.

Chances are you are building something that has an interesting team of people to back it up. In such scenarios, web development teams have chosen to go with testing, or even unstable, in order to get the latest software available. In other cases, conservative teams or groups with less savvy staff have resorted to stable because it's consistent for years.

It is up to you to choose between any, but this book will get you started with stable. You can change your **Advanced Packaging Tool** (**APT**) configuration later and upgrade to testing and unstable, but the initial installation media that we will use will be stable. Also, it is important that developers target the production environment as closely as possible. If you use stable for production, using stable for development will save a lot of time debugging mismatches.

You should know which versions of programming languages, modules, libraries, frameworks, and databases your application will be targeting, as this will influence the selection of your branch. You can go to `packages.debian.org` to check the versions available for a specific package across different branches. Choosing testing (outside a freeze period) and unstable will also mean that you'll need to have an upgrade strategy where you continuously check for new updates (with tools such as cron-apt) and install them if you want to take advantage of new bug fixes and so on.

How to do it...

Debian offers a plethora of installation methods for the operating system. From standard CDs and DVDs, Debian also offers reduced-size installation media, bootable USB images, network boot, and other methods. The complexity of installation is a relative factor that usually is of no concern for DevOps since installation only happens once, while configuration and administration are continuously happening.

Before you start considering replication methods (such as precooked images, network distribution, configuration management, and software delivery), you and your team can choose from the following installation methods:

- ▶ If you are installing Debian on a third-party provider (such as a cloud vendor), they will either provide a Debian image for you, or you can prepare your own in virtualization software and upload the disk later.
- ▶ If you are installing on your own hardware (including virtualized environments), it's advisable to get either the netinst ISO or the full first DVD ISO. It all depends on whether you are installing several servers over the course of several months (thus making the DVD obsolete as new updates come out) or have a good Internet connection (or proxies and caching facilities, nearby CDNs, and so on) for downloading any additional packages that the netinst disk might not contain.

In general, if you are only deploying a handful of servers and have a good Internet connection at hand, I'd suggest you choose the amd64 netinst ISO, which we will use in this book.

There's more...

There are several other points that you need to consider while choosing the right flavor of Debian. One of them is the architecture you're using and targeting for development.

Architectures

There are tens of computer architectures available in the market. ARM, Intel, AMD, SPARC, and Alpha are all different types of architectures.

Debian uses the architecture codenames i386 and amd64 for historical reasons. i386 actually means an Intel or Intel-compatible, 32-bit processor (x86), while amd64 means an Intel or Intel-compatible, 64-bit processor (x86_64). The brand of the processor is irrelevant.

A few years ago, choosing between the two was tricky as some binary-only, non-free libraries and software were not always available for 64-bit processors, and architecture mismatches happened. While there were workarounds (such as running a 32-bit-only software using special libraries), it was basically a matter of time until popular software such as Flash caught up with 64-bit versions—thus, the concern was mainly about laptops and desktops.

Nowadays, if your CPU (and/or your hypervisor) has 64-bit capabilities (most Intel do), it's considered a good practice to use the amd64 architecture. We will use amd64 in this book. And since Debian 7.0, the multiarch feature has been included, allowing more than one architecture to be installed and be active on the same hardware.

While the market seems to settle around 64-bit Intel processors, the choice of an architecture is still important because it determines the future availability of software that you can choose from Debian. There might be some software that is not compiled for or not compatible with your specific architecture, but there is software that is independent of the architecture.

DevOps are usually pragmatic when it comes to choosing architectures, so the following two questions aim to help you understand what to expect when it comes to it:

1. Will you run your web applications on your own hardware? If so, do you already have this hardware or will you procure it?

   ❑ If you need to procure hardware, take a look at the existing server hardware in your datacenter. Factors such as a preferred vendor, hardware standardization, and so on are all important when choosing the right architecture. From the most popular 32- or 64-bit Intel and AMD processors, the growing ARM ecosystem, and also the more venerable but declining SPARC or Itanium, Debian is available for lots of architectures.

   ❑ If you are out in the market for new hardware, your options are most likely based on an Intel- or AMD-compatible, 32- or 64-bit, server-grade processor. Your decisions will be influenced by factors such as the I/O capacity (throughput and speed), memory, disk, and so on, and the architecture will most likely be covered by Debian.

2. Will you run your web applications on third-party hardware, such as a **Virtual Private Server** (**VPS**) provider or a cloud **Infrastructure as a Service** (**IaaS**) provider?

   ❑ Most providers will provide you with prebuilt images for Debian. They are either 32- or 64-bit, x86 images that have some sort of community support—but, be aware they might have no vendor support, or in some cases waive warranties and/or other factors such as the SLA.

   ❑ You should be able to prepare your own Debian installation using virtualization software (such as KVM, VirtualBox, or Hyper-V) and then upload the virtual disk (VHD, VDI, and so on) to your provider.

Installing Debian GNU/Linux (Simple)

Once you choose the right installation method for Debian, you're ready to fire up the Debian-Installer. During installation you will also execute the initial configuration, and you will need to decide on several important factors of your setup, such as partitioning.

Getting ready

Before you start to install Debian, you will need to decide how you want to partition your disks. There are several reasons why one would like to partition disks beyond the **canonical** one-partition approach, most likely for security or specialized storage reasons. Also, if you will be using SAN/NAS dedicated hardware, the setup can be either simplified or made more complex.

Debian, like several POSIX-compliant operating systems and some other Linux distributions, follows the FHS or Filesystem Hierarchy Standard and you can expect configuration files in /etc, system files in /usr and /lib, variable files in /var, and so on.

There might be some discrepancies, though. FHS calls for /srv for server roles, but most installations sit variable files in /var. Static files, application files, and even database files all sit there. Thus, you might want to put /var on a different partition if you have advanced partitioning or permission needs. You could even partition out /var/lib/mysql for the MySQL database files, /var/www for the static and application files (the WWW/Document Root folder), and so on, like we will do as an example in this book using **Logical Volumes** (**LVM**).

Logical volumes will enable you to create more flexible data containers on top of concepts you already know: disks and partitions. Those flexible data containers created by logical volumes can expand different partitions in different disks and are easier to manage, resize, and move. But it can also add management overhead, and will require a more complex set up for clustering.

By **granular** we mean the ability of setting different behaviors on different partitions depending on the use case. For example, a system administrator can partition out /var/ mail to set ACLs/quotas and so on, DevOps might want to partition out /var to set security flags such as noexec (no executable files, which is OK in your web application since processes outside /var actually run your application), nodev (no special device files), and nosuid (no auto-escalation files) or remove filesystem attributes that impact performance (such as time), among others.

Here's a list of flags and their impact on partitioning:

Flag	Description
nodev	Does not interpret any special files for devices (character or block special files)
nosuid	Does not allow files that enable user or group impersonation (for example, running as root)
noexec	Does not allow execution of binaries in the filesystem, useful not only for public access partitions such as /tmp, but also anywhere for executables that don't make sense (such as pure web apps!)
noatime	Does not update the access times on the inodes of the filesystem, making access faster for servers with lots of small, heavily accessed files

Other directories that you might want to partition out are /tmp, which will inevitably store temporary files generated by your framework, your application server and other services, making the noexec/nodev/nosuid combo is very popular in this case to prevent the execution of potentially malicious files, along with dedicated disk space monitoring to prevent the partition from filling out, which can stop the server altogether.

In other scenarios (such as the mail server we talked about earlier), people will find great value in partitioning out /home, as they will be able to set ACLs and quotas and manage space much easier. But in a web application server scenario, while you are free to continue partitioning (Debian will partition out the swap space and /boot for you), the benefit you can get from continuing to do so (/usr, /etc, and so on) is arguable and can add unnecessary complexity.

How to do it...

Once you've decided on whether you want to partition out things or not, how you will split disk space, which flags/policies you will set to each partition and whether you'll use RAID, LVM, and any other technique (SAN/NAS, and so on), you can follow these steps to install Debian:

1. Go to www.debian.org/distrib/netinst, and choose **amd64** under **Small CDs**. The ISO file will download. You can now burn the ISO to a CD/DVD (if you need a physical disk to install), or boot your hypervisor with this ISO file. Since Debian 7.0, ISO files can also be written to USB media, and you can find specific images for previous releases under the hd-media folders. There are installation instructions on the installation manual available at http://www.debian.org/releases/stable/installmanual; alternatively, you can create a bootable USB from the netinst ISO using UNetbootin.

2. Fire up your server, and put the netinst disk in your CD/DVD unit. Reboot your server and follow the onscreen instructions (or manual instructions) to boot from CD/DVD. Debian will greet you with the following screen:

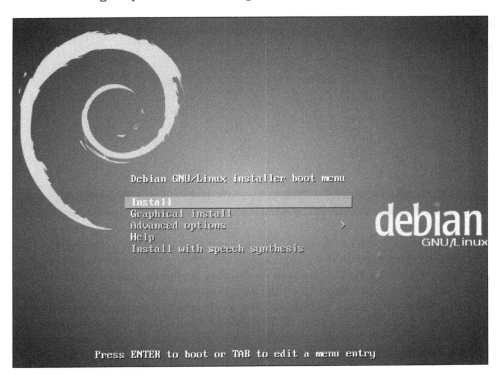

3. Hitting *ENTER* will suffice. The Debian installation will start, and you will be guided through a series of prompts (leveraging a technology called debconf) that will help you install and perform the initial setup of your installation. You might choose **Graphical install**, which will run you through the same prompts but with mouse support, colors, buttons, and scrollbars. In both modes, you can use keyboard shortcuts to make things easier (for example, in the following screen, pressing S to go for **Spanish** from a list of languages, using *Home/End/Page Up/Page Dn*, and so on).

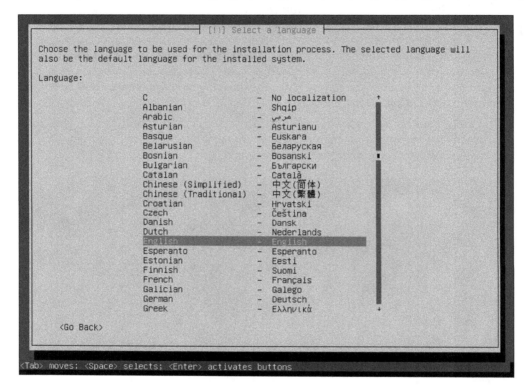

4. Choose the installation language. You can just hit *Enter* if you want **English**. Debian prides itself on having an installer available in several languages. Your selection will also hint the installer on the default country, mirrors, and time zones. Depending on your location you may want to adjust the following screens. Pay special attention to time zones, as time keeping and proper hostnames are essential to a properly functioning Linux server. Your selection will also define the keyboard layout. For example, non-English speaking people using the Latin alphabet might choose **US – International**.

5. Now, Debian will check for network connectivity. Particularly, it tries to get an IPv4 address from a DHCP server. This might not be your scenario, as DHCP servers are not usually deployed on web application environments. The operation will time out, and you will be asked to configure your network interface: IP address for the server, network mask, gateway, and DNS servers. The screen will be similar to the following screenshot:

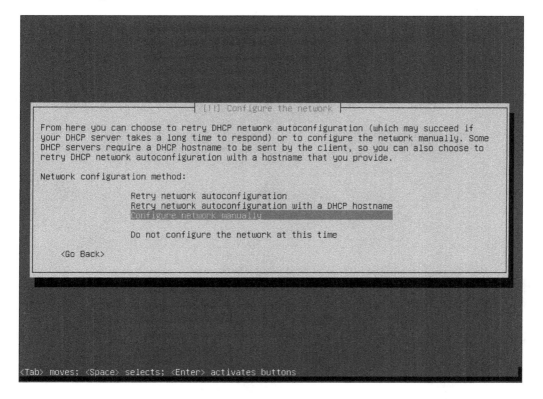

6. The next step is the hostname/domain prompt. As mentioned before, this is an important part, as you want to construct a **Fully Qualified Domain Name** (**FQDN**) that looks like `foo.bar.com`, where `foo` is your hostname and `bar.com` is your domain name. You don't need to **own** bar.com—and if you do, the IP addresses don't need to match or even exist in your DNS zone. Although it is highly recommended to use a real FQDN—both for troubleshooting and for performance reasons. You need to have the FQDN as you will use it later for network troubleshooting, clustering, copying files, and so on; if it is not configured correctly, it can be the source of lots of headaches. Large server setups use nomenclature to pinpoint the server they are managing later (such as, www-mia-01 or db-pdx-05). The input screen for the hostname is shown as follows:

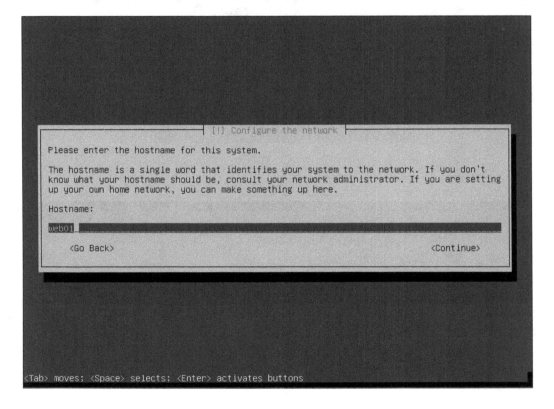

And similarly, for FQDN, as shown in the following screenshot:

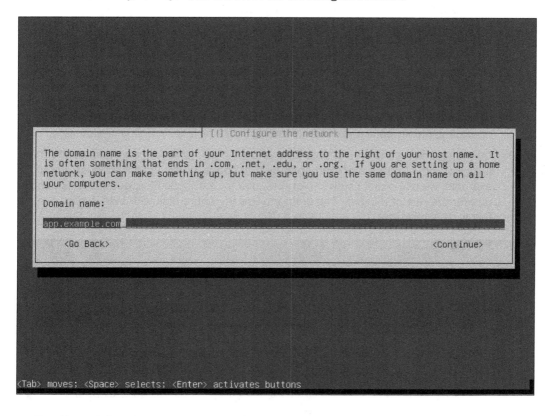

```
                    ┤ [!] Configure the network ├

  The domain name is the part of your Internet address to the right of your host name.  It
  is often something that ends in .com, .net, .edu, or .org.  If you are setting up a home
  network, you can make something up, but make sure you use the same domain name on all
  your computers.

  Domain name:

  app.example.com

      <Go Back>                                                            <Continue>



<Tab> moves; <Space> selects; <Enter> activates buttons
```

7. Next, define the root (administrator or superuser) password. You should pick a complex one, even if it's hard to remember, since you will not be using it on a day-to-day basis and will most likely be using `sudo` instead—a delegation mechanism. And you will also define an initial user with no special permissions (but basic device access)—go ahead and put in generic information if you like but still protect the account with a strong password as this user will be able to login via **Secure Shell** (**SSH**) and execute commands on a shell, which in a web application scenario are all potential points of entry. We will use DevOps.

8. It's time for partitioning. With the information gathered at the preparation stage, you will now define partitions either manually (most likely) or by using the guided mode. In the guided mode, it will be easier for you to set up, say LVM, but you will wind up with only three choices: all in one partition, separate /home, or separate /home, / usr, /var, and /tmp—and as mentioned before, you might not want to split /home and /usr. You can always delete those partitions and give space back to /var and / tmp (/tmp could be a couple of GB unless you have a hungry app in which case you should watch tmpfs memory usage). Also, you can always change the partitions (and even partition from scratch with resizing and everything) when the system is already operating, ideally before you start throwing data into it.

9. Our suggestion is that you choose LVM and all in one partition, and then delete the logical volume for root and start splitting that space in new logical volumes. In our example, we use one for web server files, one for database files, one for /tmp, and one for the rest of the disk. The option to use the entire disk with LVM is shown in the following screenshot:

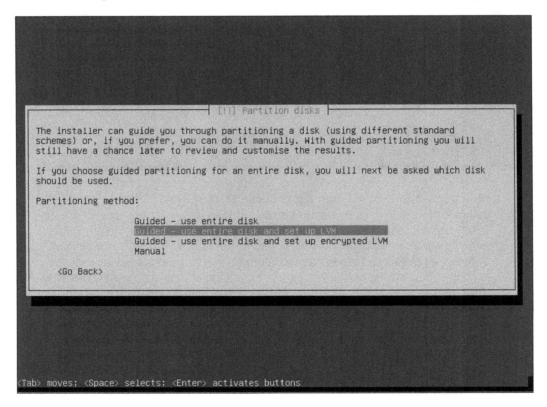

10. And, similarly, to use a single partition, as shown in the following screenshot:

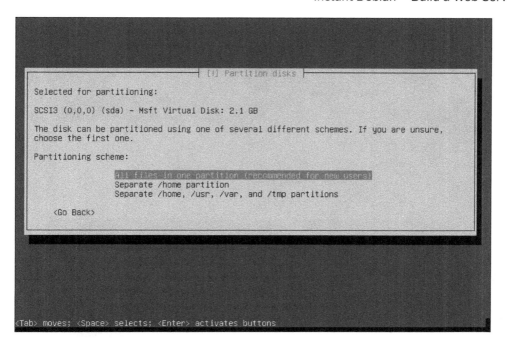

11. You can then delete the logical volume and start creating new ones as shown in the following screenshot:

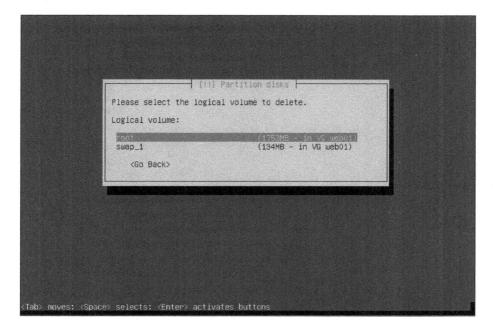

12. Also, start creating new ones in the main volume group that is remaining, as shown in the following screenshot:

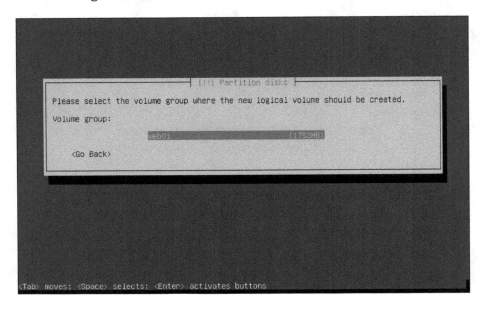

13. You can set partition options individually per each logical volume/partition you create for /tmp, as shown in the following screenshot:

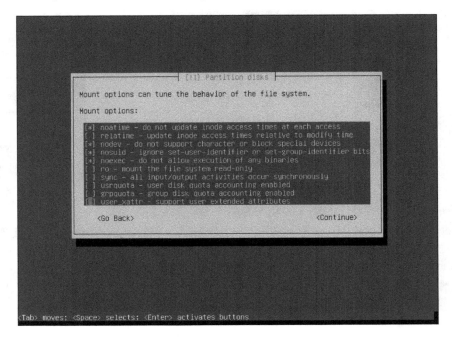

Here's a recap table with our choices for future reference:

Partition	Size	Flags	Reserved space
/var/lib/mysql	Large enough for your projected tables, indices, and so on	nodev nosuid noexec Optimized for large files	None
/var/www	Large enough for your application scripts and static files	nodev nosuid noexec noatime	None
/tmp	If you are writing hundreds of MB here, you could start using other partitions	nodev nosuid noexec noatime Optimized for small files (might vary)	None
/boot	Large enough for the projected operating system size. The final size of / after all software in the book was installed is less than 850 MB.	None (/boot contains the kernel and initrd files and unless you plan on collecting kernels lower than 100 MB for it can be enough)	5 percent (default)

14. The partitioning also involves the initial formatting of the partitions. Since wheezy (Version 7.0,released in May 2013 `http://www.debian.org/releases/stable/amd64/release-notes/`), Debian will use the ext4 filesystem by default, but you can change that to any other supported filesystem of your preference. There's a sweet spot right now with the amount of innovation happening on storage hardware and the amount of innovation happening on filesystems. Your application will, most likely, be I/O bound, meaning that better disk architectures (caches, speed, data distribution, underlying technologies, and so on) will contribute to better performance and scalability.

After partitioning and formatting, Debian is ready to install the operating system and initial software to the disk.

There's more...

If you are using the netinst disk, you will be prompted to use an online repository (mirror) that will most likely be preselected based on your country selections. You can choose one if you configured your network interfaces correctly, or you can skip it at any time (a nice trick is to use *Esc* to go to the upper menu on any function) and just install the basics that come with the netinst disk.

If you successfully selected and have access to a public Internet repository (archive), the installer will prompt you about installing tasks, which are basically families of packages that are precategorized for simplicity. Netinst doesn't actually carry many tasks because the disk itself does not carry many packages; however, just for reference, the Web server task installs Apache while the Database task installs PostgreSQL for you. Otherwise you'll be OK with the Standard System Utilities task.

Also, you will be asked to opt in to popcon, an anonymous survey where the packages you use and install are sent to Debian anonymously for statistical purposes. We suggest you choose the default (opt out) especially to avoid outgoing traffic from your production servers, but if you want to help the Debian Project know better the profiles of installed computers all over the world, the egress is just a few kilobytes a day.

You are almost set. The final question of any Debian installation is whether you want to install the GRUB boot loader or not (you might be using your own, or a particular architecture) which you do, so just press *Enter*. Installation will wrap up and reboot (the disk may be ejected, if not, eject it yourself), and the server will boot into your new system after a brief wait on the GRUB menu (you can press *Enter* to skip). The init system will kick in and you will be facing a login prompt with your hostname after a few seconds. Type in `root` and your password, and you will be facing a brand-new dash prompt. Welcome!

Making Debian GNU/Linux installations scalable (Medium)

10 years ago, Debian was not regarded as an easy-to-install distribution, and had a negative aura of exclusivity around it. And while the installation process is fairly simple, you would guess it's a pain to repeat it as is for tens or hundreds of servers.

Getting ready

There are several options for you to make the installation scale:

- Rolling out your own installation media
- Installing via the network
- Installing via the imaging server
- Preseeding the installation

How it works...

Rolling out your own installation media (remastering) involves knowledge of APT repositories, ISO 9660 structures, and preseeding. The purpose of remastering is basically adding the packages you need and your initial configuration decisions, putting them together on a media that will save time during installation. As all these steps are beyond the scope of this book, we'll point you to helpers such as live-scripts and UCK.

The second option, installing via network, is covered in detail in the Debian Installation Guide and might save some time as per running around the datacenter with optical media. As per imaging servers, SystemImager and Clonezilla are popular solutions, especially when the hardware matches in terms of disk sizes, and so on. The idea here is to install the system first, configure it, and then create an image to replicate to other servers. With imaging, be aware that you need to change the hostname—in `/etc/hosts` and `/etc/hostname` using the `hostname` command—and any other system-specific data.

How to do it...

Preseeding is one of the faster ways to save time during Debian installation. As with remastering, you install one system, and you extract the answers to the configuration prompts handled through the `debconf` program in order for them to be reused in a new installation.

1. You can also create your own preseed files by specifying as many answers as you need using standard tools:

    ```
    apt-get install debconf-utils

    debconf-get-selections -installer >preseed.cfg
    ```

2. Inspect the contents of this file with your favorite editor (`editor preseed.cfg`). You will find that questions that were asked on the installer are preceded by **#** and your answers are below. Some answers, such as password, are not included. Also, there are a lot of answers that you don't even remember to be asked about—those are defaults. Finally, you will notice that there is no answer for your partitioning elections, on the basis that you might have different servers with different hardware and different storage to address.

3. Once you have a preseed file that works, instead of selecting the **Install** option of Debian, you can choose **Advanced options**, and then **Automated install** to specify the URL of your preseed file. Probably, you will find the easiest way to do this is to serve it from another web server.

4. You can also feed broader choices, not only install-time choices, using `debconf-get-selections` without the `-installer` flag. It is useful to capture these choices at the end of your configuration process (that is, when you're done with this book).

    ```
    debconf-get-selections> package-choices.log
    ```

There's more...

The output of these tools can be fed back to the installer or to the system at any moment with the preceding steps. Notice that there are some system aspects that are not necessarily controlled by `debconf` options. For example, the contents of your Apache or MySQL configuration files are mostly edited manually and don't get registered in `debconf`.

Debian's online documentation and reference manual contain deep references to several preseeding options as well as large preseeding files that you can edit:

- ▶ `http://www.debian.org/releases/stable/amd64/ch04s05.html.es`
- ▶ `http://d-i.debian.org/manual/en.i386/apb.html`

Preparing the APT packaging system for your environment (Simple)

APT is a mature part of Debian that became the distribution's most important differentiator for years, enabling hundreds of derivative projects, including Ubuntu. Since free software is distributed by multiple parties, not always in full coordination in terms of packaging formats, release dates, versioning, configuration files, and so on, distributions are expected to put together the broadest set of software that makes sense for most users in a consistent way.

APT provides an easy, robust way for users to install software and have Debian take care of pulling software from Internet mirrors, sorting out dependencies and conflicts, installing the software and making basic configuration choices. That's why it's important.

Getting ready

The main configuration file for APT is `/etc/apt/sources.list`. In this file you define whether to use binary and source packages, whether to receive security updates and which branch and sections the system uses: main, which has most packages and consists exclusively on free software; contrib, which has software that depends on proprietary software, and non-free, which has redistributable proprietary software that Debian has decided to distribute.

How to do it...

Using your text editor, open `/etc/apt/sources.list` and review the following steps for setting up APT:

1. For most web server scenarios, you won't need source repositories, nor contrib and non-free, and you will want to make sure you receive security updates. So, `/etc/apt/sources.list` might look as simple as:

    ```
    deb http://ftp.us.debian.org/debian/ wheezy main
    deb http://security.debian.org/ wheezy/updates main
    ```

2. Changes to this file are not immediately applied. You need to update your APT system, that is, go online and grab the latest list of available software and updates. You achieve that by using the apt-get tool as follows:

    ```
    apt-get update
    ```

3. If you chose a mirror while installing Debian (using netinst), and you have Internet access at that time, this file will be prepopulated for you. If you didn't chose a mirror, you will have the CD as your first repository and `security.debian.org` as your second. In that case, you can wipe the file and use the notation indicated previously.

There's more...

There are other configuration options for APT, such as proxies and pinning/preferences, and other operations, such as a system-wide upgrade. These are rarely needed on a production system (things like pinning will be useful but are outside of the scope of this book). We will cover some of them later, but the above steps would suffice to have a configured APT system.

Also, bear in mind that there are two mainstream tools used to operate the APT system: apt-get and aptitude. We like to think that they're pretty interchangeable but advanced users will develop strong attachments to either one, and you definitely want to standardize from the beginning. This also responds to cycles, five years ago the aptitude was big because of a smarter resolution of dependencies, and so on, and it seems that apt-get has gained traction in the last year or so, mainly driven by Ubuntu. The author was a strong aptitude advocate but finds himself using apt-get lately, especially for this book.

While operations such as install, remove, update, and dist-upgrade are fairly similar in both systems, aptitude has a better search facility (aptitude search [term]) and an interface that can be useful for handling broken package situations (just type aptitude).

Installing your application platform stack (Simple)

Unless you were using the tasks mentioned in the installation recipe, you now have a properly configured server. To make it a web server, you need to install the web server, the database (if you will be hosting one), the programming language/environment, libraries, any web frameworks you're using, and so on. Fortunately, Debian packages several of them for you, and since you have a configured APT system, you can get started faster.

How to do it...

Although there are a handful of web servers packaged for Debian, there are two schools: Apache and Nginx. They have different execution models—while Nginx is a lightweight, event-oriented server that runs your application via CGI asynchronously, Apache is full of features, more mature with a thread/process approach. You can also have a dual approach where Nginx, designed for concurrency, takes the frontend paired with memcached, and Apache serves the application in the backend.

1. In either case, you will need to install the web server using APT.

   For Apache:

   ```
   apt-get install task-web-server #
   ```

   For Nginx:

   ```
   apt-get install nginx #
   ```

2. If you install Apache, you will note there are several flavors of it available as different packages; worker is one of the **MPM**s (**Multi Processing Module**) for Apache. You might also want to use prefork since it provides a similar operation model to previous versions of Apache and avoids threads, which might be a problem with non-thread-safe libraries. Simply write `apt-get install task-web-server apache2-mpm-prefork+` (think of the plus sign as "I really want this package").

3. There are two steps for configuring your web server: configure your site or virtual host, and configure your application execution method.

4. Configuring virtual hosts is very easy in both Apache and Nginx. They both have `sites-available` folders (under `/etc/apache2` and `/etc/nginx` respectively) where you can drop in a bit of configuration corresponding to your host. You can then link that file to the `sites-enabled/` folder (or, for Apache, using the a2ensite/a2dissite tool) and reload your server.

   For Apache:

   ```
   service apache2 restart #
   ```

   For Nginx:

   ```
   service nginx restart #
   ```

5. Configuring the execution method for your application depends on the programming language you are using (Perl, Python, PHP, Ruby, and so on). We'll assume PHP. As previously mentioned, while Nginx will run PHP via FastCGI, Apache also offers the possibility of using `mod_php`, where PHP is basically embedded in the Apache process. For doing that, you only need to install and enable the `mod_php` module:

    ```
    apt-get install libapache2-mod-php5
    ```

    For Nginx, the easiest configuration involves spawning a PHP FastCGI process (manually or optionally with an `init` script) and setting FastCGI parameters, as described on the Nginx Wiki page (`http://wiki.nginx.org/PHPFcgiExample`). Here, you can find lots of other configuration snippets, including advanced proxying, caching, and specific directives for CMS and other programming languages besides PHP.

    Separating the database from the application server may also make sense since the database is I/O bound but the web application is not—most of the time. But you might not have much hardware, or you might be planning on scaling out with tight application plus database units in volumes. Or you might not be using a conventional database at all. However, let's assume you are.

6. As with the application server, there are two schools for RDBMS: MySQL and PostgreSQL. Debian's default is PostgreSQL but you're free to choose.

    ```
    apt-get install mysql-server
    ```

    OR

    ```
    apt-get install postgresql
    ```

    Configuration involves lots of variables, from performance to security, and while the default configuration works fine for setting up your server, we will provide some pointers later in the book.

7. Finally, you need to install the proper bindings for the programming language you're using; otherwise, the application will not be able to connect to the database. For example:

    ```
    apt-get install php5-mysql
    ```

8. Most likely, the interpreter for your language is already installed on Debian (such as Perl, Python) or is readily available (such as PHP through `mod_php`, or Ruby, and so on) but some libraries might not be. For example, if your application needs `gd` extensions, you can perform:

    ```
    apt-get install php5-gd
    ```

While you may find frameworks such as Dancer, Rails, or Symfony conveniently packaged in Debian's repositories, they are changing creatures by nature, and most developers download them from the project's website and roll their own outside the APT system. We discuss frameworks briefly later in this book.

Setting up your storage, security, and permissions (Simple)

As mentioned earlier, partitioning is very important for a web server. You already took your first steps by selecting which directories you wanted partitioned out (hopefully, at least /tmp and /var or /var/www), but now you need to set security and permissions for them.

Getting ready

If you will have several profiles for users and groups, this is a good time to review them as you prepare to harden the storage permissions. On Unix systems, everything is a file, and a lot of the security measures depend on filesystem security.

How to do it...

At root, open /etc/fstab with a text editor. Towards the end of it, you will see lines for the partitions you created during installation.

```
/dev/mapper/web01-root /                  ext4     noatime,errors=remount-ro 0
 1
/dev/mapper/web01-tmp /tmp                 ext4     noatime,nodev,nosuid 0          2
/dev/mapper/web01-db /var/lib/mysql  ext4     noatime,nodev,nosuid,noexec 0
 2
/dev/mapper/web01-web /var/www        ext4     noatime,nodev,nosuid,noexec 0
 2
/dev/mapper/web01-swap_1 none              swap     sw              0          0
/dev/sr0          /media/cdrom0  udf,iso9660 user,noauto     0         0
/dev/fd0          /media/floppy0  auto     rw,user,noauto  0       0
```

You can see that we have the **/tmp**, **/var/lib/mysql** and **/var/www** folders partitioned out. In most cases, you won't need to mess with the first column which is the device name (the installer figured it out for you), but you must make sure that:

- ▶ The mount points are right

- ▶ The filesystem in use is the one you want (Debian uses ext4 by default, although many others are available)

- ▶ The mount options are right: **noatime** or **relatime** (doesn't write to the disk every time the access time changes, which speeds things up. Frankly it's not very useful on web servers, although some Unix tools will expect this behavior), **noexec** (disallows executable files), **nodev** (no special device files allowed), and **nosuid** (no files with elevation of rights enabled)

You will close an important set of attack vectors by applying this basic security measure, as most attackers rely on the `/tmp` folder being world writeable to drop and run malicious scripts there. Also, `/var` contains `/var/www` and `/var/lib/mysql` or `/var/lib/postgres`, which will benefit from that security measure as well.

Permissions are also important. On Debian, the Nginx and Apache processes run as a system user called www-data. This user must have read permissions for your application scripts and static files that most likely will be sitting on `/var/www`. But unless your application allows uploads or edits to that folder, you don't need write permissions. The following two operations can help you reset permissions:

```
chown -R www-data:www-data /var/www # resets owner and group to www-data
chmod -R a-w /var/www # removes write permissions for all users on
www-data
```

For MySQL and PostgreSQL, Debian usually defaults to the right thing (`/var/lib/mysql` is owned by MySQL) when it comes to storage permissions.

Setting up your database/data storage (Medium)

Database configuration involves lots of variables, from performance to security, and although the default configuration works fine for setting up your server, there are some bits that will need your intervention.

Getting started

Debconf will ask you some questions about databases, such as the root password for MySQL; however, if you are really into tuning, you will need to dive into the configuration files and documentation. Also notice that MySQL users are different (even if identically named) than system users.

You should also have a working knowledge on how your application consumes data, so you can choose the right performance improvement paths. In the appropriate recipes, this book will cover some pointers for logging and performance.

How to do it...

The following steps will guide you through the creation and set up of a new database:

1. You can go ahead (as a root user) and create a new database on MySQL, for example:

    ```
    mysql -u root -p # type in your password
    CREATE DATABASE book;
    ```

2. And create a new user called `book`, with password `book` that can execute all operations on all (current and future) tables of this new database, for example:

```
GRANT ALL ON book.* TO book@localhost IDENTIFIED BY 'book';
```

Or with Postgres, as the postgres (administrative, equivalent to root in Unix) user:

```
su - postgres
createuser -P book
createdb -O book book
```

The `GRANT` statement above is not a good idea in production. Can you spot why? First of all, the password is weak—although MySQL will only allow local connections to it, an attacker might plant a password cracker remotely. Second, we're granting `ALL` privileges to a single user, which is not a proper etiquette; we could restrict it only to `SELECT`, `INSERT`, and `UPDATE`, and your application could track the state of records to avoid performing `DELETE`, for example. Similarly, notice that the `-O` option in `createdb` for PostgreSQL sets the book as the DB owner, effectively giving the user privileges such as destroying objects.

This username and password is the one that you will provide to application developers to connect the application to the database. Notice that while it's possible to pass the end user credentials from the application to the database for logging (thus having deeper audit capabilities on the database), it is also complex to set up—the fastest way usually involving the PAM configuration which is beyond the scope of the book.

1. Using `mysql -u book -p <database>` or `su - book` and then `psql<database>`, you can access the interactive terminals for both MySQL and PostgreSQL. Similar commands to access the console are available for other DBs such as SQLite or MongoDB.

2. Your DBAs may also provide you with an archive file, a dump file, or a schema file, which you are expected to load into the database. Small schemas (usually with lots of `CREATE TABLE` statements) can usually be copy pasted into the interactive terminal. Larger schemas, or large dump files (with initial data such as `INSERT` statements) may need to be loaded via the command line, for example:

```
mysql -u root -p book <book.sql
psql book <book.sql
```

 You can also use in-console commands, such as `\i book.sql` for PostgreSQL or `source book.sql` for MySQL.

In PostgreSQL, archives also exist which are a more packetized way of distributing a full snapshot of the database. These are produced with `pg_archive` and restored with `pg_restore`. You can learn more about backup and restore later in this book.

By default, both MySQL and PostgreSQL will generate sockets that your application can use to access the database. This works well for local applications, but if you are separating your DB and your application, you will need to set up networking and access control.

1. Edit MySQL's configuration file and allow MySQL to listen on external interfaces:

   `editor /etc/mysql/my.cnf`

   Find the bind-address directive and change to the IP address

   - `service mysql restart`

2. Edit PostgreSQL's access configuration file and allow PostgreSQL to accept authenticated connections over the network:

   - `editor /etc/postgresql/9.1/main/postgresql.conf`
   - Add a line of the type `host book all 172.16.0.2/32 md5`, where `host` means the directive applies to remote hosts, `book` is the database name the directive applies to, `all` means any user correctly identified will be granted access, `172.16.0.2/32` is the IP address of the application server, and, `md5` means MD5 password authentication will be used.

3. Now reload PostgreSQL with `service postgresql reload`.

Configuring your programming language libraries (Medium)

Frameworks are very popular nowadays. Symfony, Rails, Django, or Dancer are all references for professional web development, and a Debian web server is no stranger to them. The libraries and modules that empower these frameworks are also popular, and it's important for system administrators to know how to set it up.

Getting started

You have the option to use prepackaged frameworks or downloading and installing it yourself. The prepackaged frameworks may offer ease of set up and administration at the cost of an older version. You will also have security updates coming from the APT system itself.

How to do it...

1. Search for your library. Some PEAR libraries are available on Debian, and so are CPAN libraries for Perl, Ruby gems, Python modules, and so on. Here are some useful searches:

```
aptitude search ^php-.*
aptitude search ^lib.*-perl
aptitude search ^ruby\|libruby-.*
aptitude search ^python-.*
```

2. In other cases you have the pear, rubygem clients available for manual installs (CPAN comes with Debian).

```
apt-get install php-pear
apt-get install rubygems
```

3. Here's an example, using the Dancer framework:

```
sudo apt-get install libdancer-perl
sudo editor app.pl and type:
use Dancer;
get '/demo' => sub { "Dancer is OK" };
dance;
perl app.pl
```

4. Now use a browser to go to `http://localhost:3000` (or use `wget` or `curl` on the console) to check whether the framework is working correctly.

Setting up secure remote support options (Simple)

Most DevOps manage their servers remotely using SSH. Of course there are other options, such as web-based management interfaces (like Webmin) and graphical interface management options, such as **Virtual Network Computing** (**VNC**), **Remote Desktop Protocol** (**RDP**), and TeamViewer. In this recipe, we'll go through SSH as a more secure and productive way that we suggest for secure remote management and support.

Getting started

Consistent with the practice of reducing the attack surface by shutting down unused services, graphical user interfaces and remote desktop services are usually considered bad practice on web servers. That's why SSH is king. Web-based management interfaces might be useful, but they can also pose security risks. If you decide to implement any of these solutions, you should have clear firewall restrictions in place and keep your software up-to-date.

Also, there's an important consideration regarding identity management on production servers. When your support team grows, you'll want to have audit capabilities built-in for your employees (and it might also be required by your company's security policies/practices as well as industry regulations), so this recipe will cover it as well.

How to do it...

1. Install the OpenSSH server by using the command `apt-get install ssh`; among other things, this will generate a set of keys for your OpenSSH server. You should take note of them the first time you connect to the server as they will help you verify whether you're remotely connecting to the right server (and OpenSSH clients will warn you if those fingerprints change).

2. Now, from a remote server or client (including PuTTY or Cygwin on Windows) run `sshroot@web01.app.example.com`; you should receive a fingerprint warning (which you should double-check and accept if correct), and then you will be presented with a prompt.

3. The defaults for OpenSSH are OK for most setups. You might want to change banners or ports as necessary. The reason why people change SSH's default port (TCP 22) is because it's widely known and scanned on IPv4 subnets. If you have a dedicated security hardware in place and/or will not expose the port to globally routable IPv4 networks, you might as well leave the default.

4. There is one exception though. OpenSSH is allowing root to login, which is not considered a good practice.

5. Fire up your editor and make changes to `/etc/ssh/sshd_config`; search for the `PermitRootLogin` directive and change it to `no`.

6. Then restart OpenSSH by using the command `service ssh restart`.

7. Actually, using `root` for administrative purposes is also not seen as a good practice. You should use `sudo`, which will enhance your audit capabilities and eventually allow better privilege separation using the command `apt-get install sudo`.

8. We will make a simple change with the existing non-privileged user we created that goes a long way for security in terms of audit and skill building.

9. To do so, use the command `usermod -aG sudo devops`.

10. By adding `devops` to the `sudo` group, they will be able to use `sudo` to escalate. This is only a first step that provides better insights and practices for audit, but you need to granularize `sudo` per user as necessary and not see it as a drop-in root replacement—in which case you would only have achieved minimal auditing capabilities and no real positive security outcomes.

11. Now type `exit` (or press *Ctrl+D*) to exit the root login, and login as `devops`.

12. Prepend `sudo` to the commands that need administrative privileges from now on. You will be asked for your password once in a while for added security. You can now change the root password to a very long, unique, and complex password and hopefully never login as root again. From now on, the book will use the `sudo` command when needed to specify that administrative rights are needed.

Keeping your system up-to-date (Simple)

While some people would rather develop, test, and deploy only on one set of software releases and would rather not change that in years, others would like to stay on the bleeding edge of software.

Getting ready

There are two reasons why updating is important on Debian, for a production server:

▶ Patching security problems, which are usually well-known and may have exploits in the wild through package updates released by the security team and distributed through a special repository

▶ Making sure there is binary compatibility between all the packages in your system (or explicitly break it)

For example, if you were running squeeze (the previous stable version, also known as oldstable antecessor to wheezy) with applications that did not play well with PHP 5.3, you would rather explicitly break your system by having an older PHP (an older Apache, and an older MySQL for PHP library, and so on).

On the other hand, if you were running wheezy (stable) with Nginx, you would like to have the recent security updates for the web server.

It's important to remember that in some cases, upgrading your system (and especially the libraries) might involve API changes that you should be aware of. In 2012, the author released code for a Perl-based Twitter client that used the Twitter API and the POSIX and MongoDB Perl modules; the author had to change the code in 2013 because a function on POSIX was dropped and the MongoDB syntax for connecting to databases and collections changed.

How to do it...

While running stable, Debian will not usually push an update that breaks compatibility. But security updates will go through and when enough security updates are issued, those updates are moved into the main repository. Here's a good recipe for staying on top of it:

1. Install cron-apt with the command `sudo apt-get install cron-apt`.

2. By default, cron-apt is scheduled to run on a maintenance window of 4 A.M. local time; edit this with the sudo editor `/etc/cron.d/cron-apt` and change if necessary.

3. Make sure services are running after the upgrade (for example, by using a browser or database client, or following your internal test procedures).

4. If you ever need to do a manual upgrade:

    ❏ `sudo apt-get update` will connect to the Internet and download lists with new versions of software

    ❏ `sudo apt-get dist-upgrade` will upgrade the system

There's more...

A word of caution. If you're using the codename `stable` on your `/etc/apt/sources.list` file, the `dist-upgrade` command will make major changes when a new release comes out. You might want to stick with the codename `wheezy` for consistency or be on top of announcements to be prepared.

In general, upgrades within the same release are fairly safe even for a production environment. And as mentioned earlier, you might choose to not use cron-apt at all. In such cases, you might want to change the default action of cron-apt.

Bear in mind that kernel upgrades don't require an immediate restart. You might as well keep operating with the old kernel until a proper maintenance window is defined. However, very old kernels can break future upgrades of some system libraries.

Backing up your environment (Medium)

There are different types of backup. When you think of backing up your environment, it helps to think of how you want to restore it. Do you want to restore it quickly? Do you want to restore it from the bare bones? Do you want to invest more or less time doing the actual restoration process? Do you want to be granular about what you restore?

Debian has different software for all those types of backups. You should select the one that you feel comfortable with, and not try to find a feature-by-feature replica of what you had in your old environments, or try to use whatever the rest of the people are using on the Internet.

For a web server, you usually have two options: bare metal backup and restore or just web server filesystem backup and restore. The former is usually more comprehensive and complex to set up and maintain, and the latter is easier to get running but covers less recovery scenarios.

In any case, you should also add special considerations for backing up your databases and caches, as they usually store information in memory that needs to be flushed to the disk. In some cases like in Postgres (`http://stackoverflow.com/questions/1216660/see-and-clear-postgres-caches-buffers`), it is not easy to flush cache manually; you need to stop the database altogether.

In general, it's best to back up a stopped system. That's why it's important to have a scalability strategy for your application so it can keep running while you back up masters.

For the bare metal recovery solution, we'll use Bacula. We will also share some tips on how to use rsync for a web backup scenario. The reason why rsync might make sense here is that you don't have a large datacenter with lots of different servers and operating systems; most likely, you have Debian running a web application, with any number of similar hardware running slaves.

Bacula is distributed, so you can have a director, a storage daemon (server where backups are stored) and several file daemons (clients to be backed up); for the purpose of this guide, we'll consider you have the director and storage together. Also, the director can use different backends for metadata storage. It could make sense to use the same database as your web application to potentially re-use existing DBA skills. We'll use MySQL.

Besides `/var/www` and `/var/lib/mysql` or `/var/lib/postgres`, you'd usually want to back up several critical folders such as `/etc`, which contains configuration for your setup. `/var` may also be a good idea especially if you're using other caches or software with variable data. The rest of your system, particularly `/usr` and `/lib`, are usually not modified and come prepackaged on Debian packages; `/tmp` is volatile (clears out with each restart) and `/dev` is autogenerated.

Of course, if you're going with a bare metal strategy, then you recover your setup from the ground up.. More on that in the next recipe, *Restoring your environment*.

How to do it...

In this section, you will install and configure Bacula Director, Storage Daemon and Console, with a MySQL backend:

1. In your backup server, install all Bacula components using `apt-get`: `sudo apt-get install baculabacula-director-mysqlbacula-sd-mysqlbacula-console`.

2. In the sudo editor, enter `/etc/bacula/bacula-director.conf`.

3. Browse to the `Client {}` group, the first one will be the server itself, and the second one is commented out. You can uncomment it and change the directives:

    - **Name**: It should match the name in `/etc/bacula/bacula-fd.conf` of the client
    - **Address**: It is the IP address or FQDN for the client
    - **Password**: It should match the one of the client, or you can make your own

4. Also, in `/etc/bacula/bacula-sd.conf`, make sure an IP address or FQDN is used, and that the name under **Device | Archive Device** and the password matches the one in `director.conf`.

5. Restart Bacula by using the `service bacula-director restart` and `sudo service bacula-sd restart` commands.

6. In your client server (your web application server), install the Bacula file daemon components using the command, `sudo apt-get install bacula-fd`.

7. Open the `/etc/bacula/bacula-fd.conf` configuration file, set Bacula to listen on your internal backup address and set the hostname and password of the allowed director: `sudo editor /etc/bacula/bacula-fd.conf`.

8. Browse to the `Director {}` group, change **Name** to the name of the director (found under `Director/Name` in `/etc/bacula/bacula-director.conf` on the server) and take note of the password (it needs to match the one on the server).

9. Browse to the `FileDaemon {}` group, change **FDAddress** to a non-loopback IP address where the director can reach you.

10. Issue a `sudo service bacula-fd restart` command.

11. To test it on the director, run:

```
sudobconsole
status
```

Type in: 3 (for client)

Type in: 2 (usually your client will be #2)

12. Bacula will show a picture similar to the following one. You should see no error messages and no jobs running.

```
Status available for:
     1: Director
     2: Storage
     3: Client
     4: All
Select daemon type for status (1-4): 3
The defined Client resources are:
     1: bkp01-fd
     2: web01-fd
Select Client (File daemon) resource (1-2): 2
Connecting to Client web01-fd at 10.11.11.99:9102

web01-fd Version: 5.2.6 (21 February 2012)   x86_64-pc-linux-gnu debian 7.0
Daemon started 07-Jun-13 19:49. Jobs: run=0 running=0.
 Heap: heap=270,336 smbytes=15,776 max_bytes=15,923 bufs=48 max_bufs=49
 Sizeof: boffset_t=8 size_t=8 debug=0 trace=0
Running Jobs:
Director connected at: 07-Jun-13 20:00
No Jobs running.
====

Terminated Jobs:
====
You have messages.
*_
```

13. Bacula uses **FileSet**, which are lists of files and folders to backups; **Schedule**, which define when to run backups; and **Jobs**, **JobDefs**, and **JobSets** (groups of Jobs). We are going to create a simple FileSet, a simple JobDefs and a simple Job. You can copy and paste from the existing content of /etc/bacula/bacula-director.conf. The content of the **JobDefs** should look as shown in the following screenshot:

```
JobDefs {
    Name = "WebBackup"
    Type = Backup
    Level = Incremental
    Client = web01-fd
    FileSet = "Web"
    Schedule = "WeeklyCycle"
    Storage = File
    Messages = Standard
    Pool = File
    Priority = 10
    Write Bootstrap = "/var/lib/bacula/%c.bsr"
}
```

The **Job** type, on the other hand, should reference the **JobDefs** type, as illustrated here:

```
Job {
  Name = "BackupWeb01"
  Client = web01-fd
  JobDefs = "WebBackup"
}
```

And finally the **FileSet** type, which is referenced from the **JobDefs** type, should look like this:

```
FileSet {
  Name = "Web"
  Include {
    Options {
      signature = MD5
    }
    File = /var/www_
  }
}
```

14. This creates a weekly backup for **web01** that brings (incrementally) the contents of `/var/www` to the server. After setting it up, you need to issue a `sudo service bacula-director restart` command. Now in bconsole, navigate to **Status | Director** where you should see:

```
Scheduled Jobs:
Level         Type    Pri  Scheduled        Name           Volume
=====================================================================================
===
Incremental   Backup  10   07-Jun-13 23:05  BackupClient1  *unknown*
Incremental   Backup  10   07-Jun-13 23:05  BackupWeb01    *unknown*
Full          Backup  11   07-Jun-13 23:10  BackupCatalog  *unknown*
```

15. You should also label the volume using bconsole first and then the label. Pick a name for your volume (since you are using file storage, this is not incredibly important except for reference reasons) and choose the **File** pool.

16. With Bacula, you can issue manual backups when necessary using bconsole. Just use **run** and select the job you created, then hit **Yes**. The output should look as in the following screenshot:

```
*run
Automatically selected Catalog: MyCatalog
Using Catalog "MyCatalog"
A job name must be specified.
The defined Job resources are:
     1: BackupClient1
     2: BackupWeb01
     3: BackupCatalog
     4: RestoreFiles
Select Job resource (1-4): 2
Run Backup job
JobName:  BackupWeb01
Level:    Incremental
Client:   web01-fd
FileSet:  Web
Pool:     File (From Job resource)
Storage:  File (From Job resource)
When:     2013-06-07 20:03:27
Priority: 10
yes
Job queued. JobId=1
```

17. Your job should end soon, and you can check it by navigating to **Status | Director** in bconsole. An **OK** status (no errors) is pictured as shown in the following screenshot:

```
6  Full          4    68.23 K  OK      07-Jun-13 20:30 BackupWeb01
```

18. For rsync, you will also need a storage server. You can initiate the back up from either side, and the good news is that the restore works the same just by inverting some parts of the rsync command line. Let's suppose you are initiating the back up from the client (web server):

```
rsync -avz /var/www user@backup:/var/backups/webapp
rsync -avz /var/lib/mysqluser@backup:/var/backups/mysql
```

The -avz options are the most popular set of options passed to rsync. z enables compressions and a enables the archive mode that will preserve useful things such as symlinks. v is verbose and will show filenames and the sent/received tally as well as the bandwidth used.

There's more...

As mentioned before, you should be careful about data not written to disk. Here are some tips:

- Stop your database using the service `mysql stop` or `service postgresql stop`, or flush MySQL tables (`http://dev.mysql.com/doc/refman/5.5/en/backup-methods.html`) with `FLUSH TABLES tbl_list WITH READ LOCK` (remember to use `UNLOCK TABLES` after the back up) if your engine and application model supports it

- If your application does not handle database unavailability, you might have to stop your web server as well using the command, `service apache2 stop`

Alternatively, use Bacula's application-specific scripts for MySQL (`http://dev.mysql.com/doc/refman/5.5/en/backup-methods.html`), which uses full dumps (this may take a lot of time depending on your database size and uses a lot of disk I/O, which you'll definitely consume either way since you're backing up a disk)

You should also check on `bacula-director.conf` where you want your files restored. Bacula will put a dummy path (something like `/nonexistent/path/...`), but you should put something like `/var/backups/restore` or something meaningful to you. We chose `/bacula-restores`.

We suggest that Debian users back up their installed package lists and their responses to debconf, the Debian configuration interface. You can use the following to prepare a file that can be later backed up by Bacula or manually:

```
debconf-get-selections > debconf.txt
dpkg –get-selections > packages.txt
```

Restoring your environment (Simple)

A strong backup strategy only makes sense if it's easy to restore a consistent back up. The previous recipe should have provided insights on the right backup strategy from the answer to the question, how do you expect to backup? As a result, it's important that you always test your restore procedures to see whether they fit your business needs; here's a proposed one.

Getting ready

Both Bacula and rsync require that you install Debian again and set up the Bacula file daemon as explained in the corresponding recipes of this book. This is all you need to get prepared for restore.

For the Bacula example, we deleted a file from `/var/www`, and we will restore it with Bacula. For future reference, here's the MD5 of the file we're deleting:

```
root@web01:/var/www# md5sum *.*
21dde95d9d269cbb2fa6560309dca40c   index.html
root@web01:/var/www#
```

How to do it...

1. From the Storage/Director server, fire up Bacula's console `sudobconsole` and call `restore`.

2. You have several options to restore, and all of them will use the catalog to find the matching job and pool to restore from. We will choose option 5—most recent backup for the client web01-fd.

3. Bacula will match a recent `JobId` and will put you in the selection mode where you can choose which file(s) to restore. We browse to `var/www` and mark `install.log`, type **done**, and hit **yes**.

4. Now we can find `install.log` in `/bacula-restores` and move it back to `/var/www` if we decide to do so.

```
root@web01:/var/www# mv /bacula-restores/var/www/install.log .
root@web01:/var/www# md5sum *.*
21dde95d9d269cbb2fa6560309dca40c   index.html
abf1a73dc4d71419b374f281a5b9eda4   install.log
```

5. Using rsync, you just need to oppose the argument to restures. Now the backup server comes first. This is to be executed from the client machine:

```
rsync -avzuser@backup:/var/backups/webapp/* /var/www
rsync -avzuser@backup:/var/backups/mysql /var/lib
```

Preparing for common security scenarios (Medium)

Running a web server poses very specific security risks. Attackers know that web applications are powered by databases potentially containing profitable information. They also know that nowadays lots of web applications are built on top of open source frameworks, libraries, and execution environments and there's both an open and a black market for knowledge on vulnerabilities and exploits for them.

Sometimes, attackers just use sheer computing and networking power to slow your application down to a crawl by exhausting all the system resources. This is called a **Denial of Service** (**DoS**) and can evolve into a **Distributed Denial of Service** (**DDoS**) where several computers in several different networks are joining the attack. This can be a very frustrating attack, and one that can also be triggered by an unexpected growth of legitimate users.

Finally, attacks on web applications are very visible as they can usually emerge as defacements, changes in the appearance, or functionality of the application that can subject the developers to public humiliation. The exploits, and the defacements, usually manifest themselves by modifying files on the filesystem and potentially installing other malware from **Internet Relay Chat** (**IRC**) bouncers to rootkits.

Getting started

Even in such a bleak scenario, there are some steps that can be taken; for example, setting up a firewall, setting DoS/DDoS control measures, setting up a file modification watchdog, among others. We will cover some of those scenarios here for your convenience, but they are no substitute for a broader security policy and methodologies. For code security, we also refer developers to Microsoft's Security Development Lifecycle (`http://www.microsoft.com/security/sdl/resources/publications.aspx`), with several resources available under a Creative Commons license.

How to do it...

In this section, you will install a Netfilter firewall helper, configure some kernel-level security options, and install a host-based file modification detection system.

1. Install FireHOL using the command, `sudo apt-get install firehol`.
2. Run `sudofireholhelpme> /etc/firehol/firehol.conf`.
3. Review the configuration file, and now run `sudo service firehol start`.

   If your SSH server, web server, Bacula File Director, and MySQL/PostgreSQL server have been running on an external interface so far, FireHOL should pick them up and generate exceptions for them. When you run the service `firehol start`, the firewall will block everything except for connections to those ports.

FireHOL uses Netfilter (commonly known as **iptables**), and you can add/remove client/server services from the configuration file as well as add particular iptables rules.

Although there are no silver bullets for DoS/DDoS, it doesn't mean you shouldn't implement some mitigation procedures. As mentioned before, DoS works because it exhausts your system resources. If you stop allocating some of those resources, you might stay within the operating threshold. There are operating system (network stack) measures and application-level measures that chiefly deal with **Synchronize (SYN)** states, a transitional state for legitimate connections but one that attacking connections exploit.

4. Reduce the SYN timeout to get rid of those connections faster, and turn TCP SYN Cookies on to enable the system to take more connections when the SYN queue fills up `sudo editor /etc/sysctl.conf`, and add the following:

   □ `net.netfilter.nf_conntrack_tcp_timeout_syn_recv=30`

   □ `net.ipv4.tcp_syncookies = 1`

5. Changes to `sysctl.conf` can be enforced upon reboot or by running `sudo sysctl -p /etc/sysctl.conf`.

6. Create a new Netfilter chain to limit and block new SYN connections; in this case, we have a limit of 50 initial connections followed by 10 per second:

   □ `iptables -N syn-flood`

   □ `iptables -A syn-flood -m limit --limit 10/second --limit-burst 50 -j RETURN`

   □ `iptables -A syn-flood -j DROP`

7. When you create a chain, remember to pipe your traffic through this chain.

   `iptables -A INPUT -p tcp --syn -j syn-flood`

Regarding filesystem-based security scenarios, one of the main questions is how to stay on top of changes of critical system and application files, and be able to respond timely. RKHunter is a great tool that monitors common files for potential rootkit signatures or changes. It integrates very well with APT, so every time you use APT to install software, it will help you scan the system. In the case that it finds any vulnerability, it will send you a mail (you can check your mail using `sudo mail`).

```
sudo apt-get install rkhunter
```

You can also run with `sudorkhunter -c` manually.

It is recommended to run RKHunter periodically, and during installation, it also offers the possibility to integrate into the APT system (more exactly, the dpkg toolset) to provide automatic scanning during package management operations.

There's more...

With several different attack vectors in the market and several different open source countermeasures, there might be a temptation to install and run every single tool imaginable. You might want to go up the stack with solutions like mod_evasive that might help at the web server level. But beware, they may also consume large amounts of resources.

Port scanning is a common information gathering/reconnaissance practice among potential attackers. Mapping the ports that are closed, open, or filtered as well as potentially determining which services are running can save the attackers' time. And when a service like SSH has been identified, password guessing, dictionary, and brute-force attacks can be launched. While going obscure will not make you invulnerable, readily available solutions exist for services like SSH, such as fail2ban, which will preemptively cut off some automated tools executing password attacks. Installation is as easy as executing the command, `sudo apt-get install fail2ban`.

There are lots of other measures that you will need to take to secure your server. From content inspection with tools such as Snort or mod_security to passive and active measures, it can be a task of its own; unfortunately, the book does not cover all potential approaches to web application security.

Reading logs and troubleshooting your setup (Simple)

Logfiles can contain useful information for troubleshooting. For example, you might see a directive that is not correctly set up, a syntax error, or even a communications error. Then it is time to review the configuration file, correct the errors, and restart/start the service.

Getting started

From the moment you install Debian your system will start recording logs. They are sitting on `/var/log`, are rotated daily (if needed) and compressed, and you should back them up. There are system-level and application-level logs. You can even enable additional verbosity and/or debugging information by searching the configuration files for `log` directives. It is important that you familiarize yourself with the contents of `/var/log` and the files that each application and/or service generates.

How to do it...

Familiarize yourself with grep and less (`sudo apt-get install less`), which enable you to:

- Add your user to the adm group by running `sudo usermod -a -G adm devops`. The adm group will allow you to read several logfiles under the `/var/log` folder, thus reducing the need to use `sudo` for any subsequent commands.

- Search for a particular term in a file (`grep -i 'disk is full' /var/log/syslog`)

- Then use tail to monitor additions to the file, `tail -f /var/log/bacula/bacula.log`.

- The following are default logfiles that can be useful for a web server:

    - Any error 500 should be logged in `/var/log/apache2/error.log`

    - `/var/log/mysql.err` and `/var/log/mysql.log` contains MySQL logs and `/var/log/postgresql/postgresql-9.1-main.log` contains Postgres'

    - `/var/log/syslog` is very useful for networking logs as well as for **OOM**s (**out of memory**) errors

There's more...

Debian uses `logrotate` to control periodic rotation of logs. After some days of running your server, you will notice that `/var/log` starts filling up with files ending in `.0` and `.gz`. These are rotated logfiles that are archived based on time or size rules. You can move them to your backup, and `.gz` files can also be searched by using `zgrep` instead of `grep`.

Applications such as logcheck (`sudo apt-get install logcheck`) can help monitor for log anomalies. You may also want to use remote syslog servers or logging applications such as Prelude that centralize logs for several servers and help you determine the timelines of events.

Regarding timelines, it is also important to have synchronized clocks in all your servers. This is something that is easily achievable by installing the ntp daemon, `sudo apt-get install ntp`, or by using a manual tool such as ntpdate-debian, available in the ntpdate package.

Using proxies, caches, and clusters to scale your architecture (Advanced)

Eventually you'll find that you need to start splitting your application to accommodate growth. This recipe discusses some components and strategies that you might consider, including Ultra Monkey, a methodology that will help you get started navigating the different clustering components that can be used in your application.

Getting started

Chances are your setup will be more complex than a simple web plus database server. When that happens, it's time to start thinking about how to scale your architecture. You can start with simple separation (as outlined in the *Optimizing your solution performance* recipe) such as moving the databases to different servers, moving the backup components to different servers, and so on, or by splitting the application entirely.

How to do it...

In this section, you will set up Nginx as a frontend server, which queries Apache for URIs and uses Memcache to cache some responses. This will provide in-memory caching of objects, an event-based frontend, and will not require you to change your Apache configuration.

1. Change the port where Apache's running, so it doesn't conflict with Nginx:
   1. Run the command `sudo editor /etc/apache2/ports.conf`.
   2. Change **80** to `8080` in the **Listen** and **NameVirtualHost** directives.
   3. Run the command `sudo editor /etc/apache2/sites-enabled/*`.
   4. Change **80** to `8080` in the **VirtualHost** directive.
   5. Run the command `sudo service apache2 restart`.

2. Now, you can use Netfilter to avoid connections to TCP port 8080, since it will only be accessed locally by Nginx:

   ```
   sudo iptables -A INPUT -p tcp -dport 8080 -j DROP
   ```

3. Install Nginx (if it wasn't installed before) using the following steps:
   1. Run the command `sudo apt-get install nginx`.
   2. Run the command `sudo editor /etc/nginx/sited-enabled/ default`.

3. Search for the `location /` section and replace it with:

```
server {
  location / {
    set $memcached_key $uri;
    memcached_passlocalhost:11211;
    default_type          text/html;
    error_page            404 @fallback;
  }

  location @fallback {
    proxy_pass http://localhost:8080;
  }
}
```

4. Restart Nginx with `sudo service nginx restart`.

5. Install memcached with `sudo apt-get install memcached`.

6. Now you need to load objects into memcached. The key for the object is the URI; if you're trying to reach `http://example.com/icon.jpg`, and you want `icon.jpg` served from Memcache, you need to load it first. Here's a simple PHP script to do it:

```
<?php
  $mc = new Memcached();
  $mc->addServer("localhost", 11211);
  $value = file_get_contents('/var/www/icon.jpg');
  $mc->set("/icon.jpg", $value);
?>
```

You can also use memcdump or other tools to massively load objects in your Memcache. If the key is not found in Memcache, Nginx will fall back to Apache.

As mentioned before, Ultra Monkey is not a product but a methodology for setting up service clusters. It leverages existing open source technologies such as Heartbeat and Linux Virtual Server. Heartbeat provides high availability and Linux Virtual Server provides load balancing. Ultra Monkey enables different architectures or topologies (`http://www.ultramonkey.` `org/3/topologies/ha-lb-overview.html`), and we will cover the load balancing one.

You need two or more web servers to do this, and it's supposed that you're running the same application in all of them, connecting to a single database.

 This particular scenario (only two servers) actually requires more setup (ARP replies, packet forwarding) which is described in full in the Ultra Monkey page. It has been abbreviated here for space, and this procedure will work well when you have several backends and one "gateway" balancer running ldirectord. You could add Heartbeat to another gateway and have a fully available gateway director for a large number of nodes in your cluster.

1. Install LVS' ldirectord via `sudo apt-get install ldirectord`.

   Now, let's assume web01 has the IP address `10.11.11.3` and web02 has `10.11.11.99`. You need to decide in which one you will run the ldirectord software or, the virtual IP address of your cluster. In our case, we'll use `10.11.11.100` as a virtual address, and the director will be `10.11.11.99`.

2. In both nodes, enable the virtual address using an alias or by adding a new address to the existing interface, `sudo ip addr add 10.11.11.100/24 dev eth0` (this change will be temporary until you declare a new virtual interface on `/etc/network/interfaces`).

3. In your cluster director, run `sudo editor /etc/ldirectord.cf` and type in:

```
checktimeout=3
checkinterval=1
autoreload=yes
quiescent=yes

virtual=10.11.11.100:80
real=10.11.11.3:80 gate
real=10.11.11.99:80 gate
service=http
request="index.html"
receive="It works"
scheduler=rr
protocol=tcp
checktype=negotiate
checkport=80
```

   Notice that in addition to the round-robin load balancing functionality, ldirectord is also checking for the existence of `index.html` and the words "It works" inside the file (this is the default Apache index file), which can help to determine that a badly configured web server should no longer be part of the cluster.

4. Make sure ldirectord is enabled, `sudo editor /etc/default/ldirectord`.

5. Now start ldirectord using `sudo service ldirectord start`.

6. Check the configuration with `sudo ipvsadm -L -n`.

Your cluster should look as follows:

```
IP Virtual Server version 1.2.1 (size=4096)
Prot LocalAddress:Port Scheduler Flags
  -> RemoteAddress:Port          Forward Weight ActiveConn InActConn
TCP 10.11.11.100:80 rr
  -> 10.11.11.3:80               Route   1      0          24
  -> 10.11.11.99:80              Route   1      0          24
```

There's more...

There are many other approaches to proxying, clustering, and caching on Linux and Debian, both open source and proprietary, such as Red Hat Cluster Suite for applications or even OpenStack for OS-level massive clustering. Evaluate all options to find an architecture that matches not only your existing solution but potential future needs as well.

Consuming Windows Azure Cloud Services (Medium)

There are some situations where consuming external services might make technical and financial sense. And it is not a new idea. Originally people started to outsource their spam services, then entire mail servers, then storage, virtual machines, and now databases, queues, and buses, and even full platforms are being consumed from the public cloud.

Getting started

The author has consumed Azure from Debian since late 2009 through the PHP SDK POC (http://bureado.com/2010/03/30/una-breve-poc-del-sdk-de-windows-azure-para-p/). The service has come a long way since then and now offers lots of other services, including VMs and a community service called VM Depot. There are several scenarios the author is familiar with, from large enterprise PHP and PostgreSQL applications on Azure all the way to Perl and Hadoop on Azure HDInsight.

How to do it...

Now we'll explore how to upload this server to Azure. We'll assume that you were using a hypervisor (the author used Hyper-V on Windows 8) so you can export the VM.

1. Moving your infrastructure to the public cloud means you will change your networking scenario. So set DHCP as your mode for eth0 by executing `sudo editor /etc/network/interfaces`, changing **static** to **dhcp**, and deleting the rest of the lines for the eth0 interface.

2. Install python-asn1, a dependency of the Windows Azure Linux Agent using the command, `sudo apt-get install python-asn1` and grab the dpkg file for waagent 1.3.2-1 (`http://packages.debian.org/sid/amd64/waagent/download`, not available in wheezy yet) from the repositories.

3. Install waagent with `sudodpkg -I waagent_1.3.2-1_amd64.deb`.

4. Deprovision the VM with `sudowaagent -deprovision` and halt the VM with `sudo halt`.

5. Now you can export the VM into the VHD format. While it's being exported (it might take a while), you can request a certificate on your Azure portal (if you haven't, you can open a trial account for free) and upload using the csupload tool on Windows:

   ❑ `csupload set-connection "SubscriptionID=$STORAGE_SUB_ID; CertificateThumbprint=$CERT_THUMB; ServiceManagementEndpoint=https://management.core.windows.net"`

   ❑ `csupload Add-PersistentVMImage -Destination "$CONTAINER_URL/my.vhd" -Label "Debian" -LiteralPath "C:\Debian.vhd" -OS Linux`

There's more...

You can also use the Azure CLI tools to upload the VM as depicted in official tutorial videos (`http://www.youtube.com/watch?v=bDAyI0imqGE`) or you could upload your VM to VM Depot (`http://vmdepot.msopentech.com/List/Index`) which has included a Debian image.

There are other services available on Azure, such as the Active Directory and BizTalk services, queues, tables, blob storage, and Hadoop; there are other PaaS and IaaS providers, such as Amazon, Google, and OpenShift. Debian has become a mainstream distribution of choice in most of the providers, and it's important to consider what the public, hybrid, and private clouds have to offer to your web architecture.

Responding to security incidents (Advanced)

It will happen. Large market share along with insufficient security practices and attack persistency will eventually result in a security breach, especially if attackers have incentives. If you operate a low-profile CMS, most likely you will be defaced. If you operate something for profit in nature, attackers might go for passwords or sensitive data. In other cases, your server may be compromised and used as a platform for other attacks, such as DDoS botnets.

You will notice defacements, strange files lying around your filesystem, processes that you know nothing about running, and so on. Those are clear signs that something is going on; although, there might be others, and for a while, there might be none making operations even more important.

Getting ready

There are two schools for responding to a security incident: shutting the power off or not. Among other things, it depends on whether you or your company prosecute violators. Although not everyone wants to go through a legal process, learning can be a very important driver of your very own internal forensic effort.

Shutting the power off, and then cloning the disk for a forensic analysis is a common approach in those cases; although, not powering it off might help gather important live information. Also, shutting it off for forensic analysis means your time-to-recovery will be significantly higher.

How to do it...

The following is a non-authoritative, non-specific list of suggestions to respond to a security incident:

1. Don't unplug the network cable. Advanced malware, especially those installed as a result of Advanced Persistent Threats (APTs, not to be confused with the packaging systems), can inflict damage when the network goes down.

2. If you decide to shut it off, pull the energy cord. This is not a clean shutdown, and you will want to take care of any critical pending operations first. Take the disk(s) out and replicate them using read-only access, ideally using a forensics duplicator. If you don't have the hardware or the knowledge, and you want to prosecute, take it to forensic professionals.

3. Recover your server as specified in Restore your environment; however, after that, you need to find and patch whichever vulnerability led to the intrusion in the first place!

4. Examination of system logs is essential, although they might have been cleared. On a web application, you'd like to take a look at the web server logs (`/var/log/apache2/*`, `/var/log/nginx/*`), especially for any error lines that might be indicative of an application vulnerability leveraged to inject code or provoke an intrusion. Also, you want to take a look at any seemingly random garbage or erroneous requests that can evidence someone is trying to exploit an error and `/var/log/auth.log` containing authentication activity (SSH logins, and so on). In addition to this, you should also look at the `/var/log/wtmp`, `/var/log/lastlog` and `/var/log/btmp` files that can be read with the `last` and `lastlog` commands and might contain important authentication information. Database logs should also be reviewed and users (in some cases, regulatory organizations) notified of privacy breaches. Also, logs of products such as RKHunter might be helpful.

5. Finally, for critically modified information such as defaced files, you'd want to check the MAC times. When you use -1, you get the modification time of a file but by adding -c, you can check the creation time and with -u, the access (use) time. Specialized forensic toolkits, such as The Coroner's Toolkit, will help you detect mismatches and timelines if necessary.

6. In most cases, if you're using a CMS or some other prepackaged web software, you can upgrade your software, themes, and modules (especially third party modules) and check on specialized mailing lists (such as full disclosure) if there are any known security vulnerabilities. Upgrading your operating system to patch any potential vulnerability is also advised.

Monitoring your server's operation (Medium)

Monitoring is a part of any operation management practice. As with any other monitoring discipline, you will need to choose which Key Performance Indicators (KPIs) are applicable to your business and application, and which thresholds/ranges are acceptable and unacceptable for you.

Getting ready

Yes, you can do real-time pedestrian monitoring by running command-line tools yourself. Let's face it, a lot of systems administrators will still login via SSH to their servers and run top for a reason; immediate snapshots have immediate value in the monitoring process. But you can also install a monitoring product and map the values over time. A mix of the two approaches will be valuable while managing a Debian system.

Some of the monitoring products out there, such as Munin, Nagios, and Zenoss, will have default values for most of the usual metrics monitored for web servers; however, you need to perform test runs that might span a couple weeks or so, with different types of loads, to understand your acceptable ranges.

How it works...

The following are some examples of KPIs for your web server on Debian:

1. Ping round-trip time (RTT), which, on a lower scale, helps determine network outages, and on a higher scale, helps understand latency issues to your server.

2. Network interface throughput, which helps understand capacity and usage.

3. Disk usage, memory usage, and CPU usage. Also, tools such as vmstat will help you do real-time analysis. The three metrics combined will help you find bottlenecks in your application, which in most cases will be I/O bound. The independent metrics will just give you an idea whether you need to add capacity or not.

4. TCP response times, which helps measure the consistency of the time the network stack takes to respond to a request on the port where your server's running (both the web and the database servers if you're using TCP connections).

5. HTTP request/response times, which helps measure the consistency of the time the web server takes to respond to a request. More advanced monitoring of this includes expected responses, specific URIs, and form workloads for testing (which may be useful for determining defacements, for example).

6. Database query response times, which helps find bottlenecks in your application. In teams with DBAs, this is usually done by the DBA as part of a performance optimization effort, but DevOps team might put that into their monitoring plate.

How to do it...

The easiest way to get a monitoring glimpse of your server's operation is to log in via SSH and interpret the output of certain commands.

1. Run vmstat. You will get a fairly cryptical snapshot of the following:

   - **procs-r**: It indicates processes waiting for runtime. It is a potential indicative of CPU-bound applications. The lower, the better—0 is best (test under load).

   - **procs-b**: It indicates processes on uninterruptible sleep which is not good. 0 is best.

   - **memory-swpd**: It indicates swapped memory. Here, 0 is normal. Having any amount here is bad because the processes will wait until the disk spins to virtual memory. You can also tweak the swappiness (tendency to swap). Swap in/swap out, the lower the better; it will be 0 if you have no swapped memory.

   - **memory-cache**: It indicates cached memory. It is generally good as it will avoid a slower I/O.

❑ **memory-free**: It indicates free memory. As opposed to Windows, Linux tends to leave free memory untouched. So it is not always an indicator of anything in particular, except if it's 0, then you're running out of memory.

❑ **Io-bi/bo**: It indicates blocks in/out of disk. Here, lower is better. High numbers here, that increase without control or patterns during loads, are indicative of an I/O-bound application. Either find the I/O bottlenecks and remove them or invest in faster storage... or a different storage architecture. Also see CPU waiting time (**wa**), which is the time waiting for I/O (here, lower is better).

❑ **cpu-us/id**: It indicates the CPU usage versus the idle time. Idle means responsiveness but also underconsumption of CPU power. A fair, consistent usage amount is a good indicator of a stable load.

2. You can use `vmstat n` to get samplings each *n* seconds. For example `vmstat 5` is good when you're doing a load test to see where your app bottlenecks are. Here is an example of a sample web server when running `httperf`. The first two samples are before the test, and the next two are during the test:

```
bureado@wietse:~$ vmstat 5
procs -----------memory---------- ---swap-- -----io---- -system-- ----cpu----
 r  b   swpd   free   buff  cache   si   so    bi    bo   in   cs us sy id wa
 0  0      0  49088  10264 243996    0    0     1     4    3   10  1  0 98  0
 0  0      0  49088  10272 243996    0    0     0     6   20   30  0  0 100  0
 3  0      0  37096  10280 243732    0    0     0    37 4070  840 31 10 59  0
 3  0      0  35080  10288 243736    0    0     0    68 4051  865 31 11 58  0
```

Can you spot the bottleneck? Yes, it's disk I/O. You can see **swap** is good, and the CPU and memory usage rates are good as well, thus no need to increase capacity.

This set up runs on a VM (particularly, a VPS), which tends to have slow storage (some people prefer to use network-based storage to avoid using the disk drivers of their hypervisors).

1. You can use jnettop (called `jnettop -i <interface name>`) to check the bandwidth usage per each TCP connection. You can see aggregates and check whether the HTTP requests or the SQL connections are using all of your available bandwidth. There are several strategies to increase the bandwidth, which we cover in this book under the *Using proxies, caches, and clusters to scale your architecture* recipe.

2. As an alternative, you can use `tcptrack` to track the TCP state as well; although, for network load, we like to use jnettop that looks like:

Client	Server	State	Idle A	Speed
64.22.71.168:1062	64.22.71.168:8000	CLOSED	0s	0 B/s
64.22.71.168:1046	64.22.71.168:8000	CLOSED	1s	67 B/s
64.22.71.168:1050	64.22.71.168:8000	CLOSED	1s	0 B/s
64.22.71.168:1044	64.22.71.168:8000	CLOSED	2s	343 B/s
64.22.71.168:1049	64.22.71.168:8000	CLOSED	1s	67 B/s
64.22.71.168:1036	64.22.71.168:8000	CLOSED	2s	276 B/s
64.22.71.168:1045	64.22.71.168:8000	CLOSED	2s	343 B/s
64.22.71.168:1041	64.22.71.168:8000	CLOSED	2s	343 B/s
64.22.71.168:1054	64.22.71.168:8000	CLOSED	1s	0 B/s
64.22.71.168:1052	64.22.71.168:8000	CLOSED	1s	0 B/s
64.22.71.168:1060	64.22.71.168:8000	CLOSED	0s	0 B/s
64.22.71.168:1051	64.22.71.168:8000	CLOSED	1s	0 B/s
64.22.71.168:1058	64.22.71.168:8000	CLOSED	0s	67 B/s
64.22.71.168:1065	64.22.71.168:8000	ESTABLISHED	0s	0 B/s
64.22.71.168:1057	64.22.71.168:8000	CLOSED	0s	67 B/s
64.22.71.168:1059	64.22.71.168:8000	CLOSED	0s	67 B/s
64.22.71.168:1047	64.22.71.168:8000	CLOSED	1s	67 B/s
64.22.71.168:1066	64.22.71.168:8000	ESTABLISHED	0s	0 B/s
64.22.71.168:1048	64.22.71.168:8000	CLOSED	1s	67 B/s
64.22.71.168:1055	64.22.71.168:8000	CLOSED	1s	0 B/s
64.22.71.168:1038	64.22.71.168:8000	CLOSED	2s	276 B/s
64.22.71.168:1061	64.22.71.168:8000	CLOSED	0s	0 B/s
64.22.71.168:1037	64.22.71.168:8000	CLOSED	2s	276 B/s
64.22.71.168:1068	64.22.71.168:8000	ESTABLISHED	0s	0 B/s
64.22.71.168:1042	64.22.71.168:8000	CLOSED	2s	343 B/s
64.22.71.168:1040	64.22.71.168:8000	CLOSED	2s	343 B/s
64.22.71.168:1043	64.22.71.168:8000	CLOSED	2s	343 B/s
64.22.71.168:1039	64.22.71.168:8000	CLOSED	2s	370 B/s
64.22.71.168:1067	64.22.71.168:8000	ESTABLISHED	0s	0 B/s
64.22.71.168:1056	64.22.71.168:8000	CLOSED	1s	0 B/s
64.22.71.168:1063	64.22.71.168:8000	CLOSED	0s	0 B/s
64.22.71.168:1064	64.22.71.168:8000	ESTABLISHED	0s	0 B/s
64.22.71.168:1053	64.22.71.168:8000	CLOSED	1s	0 B/s

```
TOTAL                                                    3 KB/s
Connections 1-43 of 43                     Unpaused  Unsorted
```

3. Previously we used `httperf` to simulate a load scenario. Now let's suppose you want to use it to actually measure the response time of your web server, simulating 10 connections using the command `httperf --hog --server=www.example.com --num-conns=10`. It should look like the following screenshot:

```
Total: connections 10 requests 10 replies 10 test-duration 4.089 s

Connection rate: 2.4 conn/s (408.9 ms/conn, <=1 concurrent connections)
Connection time [ms]: min 350.4 avg 408.9 max 485.3 median 391.5 stddev 43.0
Connection time [ms]: connect 0.2
Connection length [replies/conn]: 1.000

Request rate: 2.4 req/s (408.9 ms/req)
Request size [B]: 67.0

Reply rate [replies/s]: min 0.0 avg 0.0 max 0.0 stddev 0.0 (0 samples)
Reply time [ms]: response 408.7 transfer 0.0
Reply size [B]: header 306.0 content 0.0 footer 0.0 (total 306.0)
Reply status: 1xx=0 2xx=0 3xx=10 4xx=0 5xx=0

CPU time [s]: user 1.04 system 3.05 (user 25.5% system 74.5% total 100.0%)
Net I/O: 0.9 KB/s (0.0*10^6 bps)

Errors: total 0 client-timo 0 socket-timo 0 connrefused 0 connreset 0
Errors: fd-unavail 0 addrunavail 0 ftab-full 0 other 0
```

Our application is able to handle 2.4 req/s (given the 10 connection workload and the fact that we ran this locally), or conversely it takes 0.4 seconds to reply to one request. This operation used 0.9 KB/s of bandwidth. For production environments, you would like to set a more complex test environment with remote computers simulating hundreds or thousands of connections from different connections.

4. Measuring the response time for a SQL query is trivial. If you can write your query on the command line (for example, with `mysql -e` or `psql -c`), you can wrap the entire statement on a time call:

    `time (mysql -u root -p tsa -e 'select count(*) from token')`.

```
bureado@wietse:~$ ti
Enter password:
+-----------+
| count(*)  |
+-----------+
|        35 |
+-----------+

real    0m5.051s
user    0m0.005s
sys     0m0.008s
```

Take a look at the **user** and **sys** values—since this statement requires a password, **real** is artificially higher. Also notice that this statement will also include the time necessary to run the MySQL binary, connect, and so on, so it might be biased—for single queries, the mysql console already gives you an execution time in seconds. You could also compare the value over time by wrapping everything on a `watch` statement. But soon you will find out that the query response time depends on a lot of variables such as server load, I/O load, and so on, and that it is more efficient to focus on the queries that are systemically slow.

1. If using MySQL, edit `/etc/mysql/my.cnf` and uncomment the `log_slow_queries` directive. Queries taking more than `long_query_time` to complete will get logged to that file. Then your programmers, DBA, and you can sit and work on that query.

2. If using Postgres, edit `/etc/postgresql/9.1/main/postgresql.conf` and set `log_min_duration_statement` to a value (for example, 250ms).

3. Restart your database with the service `mysql restart` or `sudo service postgres restart` and start taking a look at the logs.

Optimizing your solution performance (Advanced)

Optimization is the next natural step of observing your server's performance. You might want to squeeze out every extra millisecond of performance, but in general, people will address optimization when there are crass performance hits on their applications.

Getting started

Without knowing it, you have probably explored performance-enhancing options already. For example, caches and load-balancing clusters, as well as cloud services, help accommodate growth, and so on. But this recipe will give you general ideas on what the common performance pitfalls are within the domain of a single server (physical or virtual), and what the low-hanging fruit for you to improve is.

How to do it...

Set up application profiling for your programming language to find bottlenecks and improve your logic. For example, Xdebug is very popular in the PHP community and can help to address some of the scenarios rapidly.

1. Install it with `sudo apt-get install php5-xdebug`.

2. Enable it for Apache with sudo editor `/etc/php5/apache2/php.ini`, browse all the way to the end, and add:

```
[xdebug]
xdebug.profiler_enable = 1
```

There's more...

5 to 10 years ago, optimizing the kernel was a big thing. People were upgrading and looking for new features to improve performance—much improvement came to laptops and desktops, and few to servers. Nowadays, lots of mid-market sysadmins prefer to leave the kernel as is in favor of eased management, while top web companies may employ teams that only do kernel optimization. Some vendors might even restrict the amount of kernel customization they can tolerate for support or warranty purposes.

Yes, faster I/O can add performance value to your server. More bandwidth, faster bus speeds, better RAM technologies, faster disks, storage using fibre, and so on should all be explored. But other solutions, such as horizontally growing by adding more servers for load balancing can also help. It is important to find the right balance between an elastic growth strategy and a manageable architecture. Fortunately, Debian has several free software tools as well as enough customization hooks for you to explore your own approach.

3. Now restart Apache with `sudo service apache2 restart`.

4. Xdebug will drop cachegrind files in `/tmp` (you can change this in `php.ini` if needed), and you can inspect those cachegrind files with a tool such as KCachegrind, which will show you the time spent on the functions as shown in the following screenshot:

Incl.	Self	Called	Function	Location
100.00	0.01	(0) {main}		alpha.php
99.99	99.99	1 php::sleep		php:internal

5. Act on your slow queries. This might mean creating indices, reviewing your data model, or ORM facilities, and even working with DBAs and developers on changing queries altogether. The next good step is to run them directly on the database console using `EXPLAIN`. `EXPLAIN` can tell you if a query is not using the most efficient way the database provides to do something; you can improve in some cases by making indices in the case of `SELECT` or provide cues for improving queries in other cases. For a simple query on a table with an index, the output looks like:

```
mysql> explain select count(*) from employees;
+----+-------------+-----------+-------+---------------+---------+---------+------+
--+--------+-------------+
| id | select_type | table     | type  | possible_keys | key     | key_len | ref
  | rows   | Extra       |
+----+-------------+-----------+-------+---------------+---------+---------+------+
--+--------+-------------+
|  1 | SIMPLE      | employees | index | NULL          | PRIMARY | 4       | NUL
L | 300584 | Using index |
+----+-------------+-----------+-------+---------------+---------+---------+------+
--+--------+-------------+
1 row in set (0.00 sec)
```

This explains the behavior of a query that is executed immediately after the server boots up, and repeated just afterwards, dropping from 0.29 seconds to execute to something much faster, as shown in the next screenshot, side by side:

```
mysql> select count(*) from employees; mysql> select count(*) from employees;
+----------+                            +----------+
| count(*) |                            | count(*) |
+----------+                            +----------+
|   300024 |                            |   300024 |
+----------+                            +----------+
1 row in set (0.29 sec)                 1 row in set (0.00 sec)
```

In this second query, **Using temporary** and **Using filesort** are not a problem when dealing with a 100-row table, but this one has 300,584, so it takes 0.23 seconds to complete.

```
mysql> select gender, count(*) from employees group by gender;
+--------+----------+
| gender | count(*) |
+--------+----------+
| M      |   179973 |
| F      |   120051 |
+--------+----------+
2 rows in set (0.23 sec)
```

EXPLAIN helped to identify the problem as indicated in the following screenshot:

```
mysql> explain select gender, count(*) from employees group by gender;
+----+-------------+-----------+------+---------------+------+---------+------+
| id | select_type | table     | type | possible_keys | key  | key_len | ref  |
rows    | Extra     |
+----+-------------+-----------+------+---------------+------+---------+------+
|  1 | SIMPLE      | employees | ALL  | NULL          | NULL | NULL    | NULL |
300584 | Using temporary; Using filesort |
+----+-------------+-----------+------+---------------+------+---------+------+
1 row in set (0.00 sec)
```

Now, by creating an index we can help the time drop (see the **Using index** clause in the following screenshot):

```
mysql> create index gender_index on employees(gender) using btree;
Query OK, 0 rows affected (2.80 sec)
Records: 0  Duplicates: 0  Warnings: 0

mysql> explain select gender, count(*) from employees group by gender;
+----+-------------+-----------+-------+---------------+--------------+---------
| id | select_type | table     | type  | possible_keys | key          | key_len
| ref   | rows   | Extra       |
+----+-------------+-----------+-------+---------------+--------------+---------
|  1 | SIMPLE      | employees | index | NULL          | gender_index | 1
| NULL | 300584 | Using index |
+----+-------------+-----------+-------+---------------+--------------+---------
1 row in set (0.00 sec)
```

Fine tuning (or tweaking) configuration parameters for cache sizes, flush behavior, and so on might also be an option.

About Packt Publishing

Packt, pronounced 'packed', published its first book "*Mastering phpMyAdmin for Effective MySQL Management*" in April 2004 and subsequently continued to specialize in publishing highly focused books on specific technologies and solutions.

Our books and publications share the experiences of your fellow IT professionals in adapting and customizing today's systems, applications, and frameworks. Our solution based books give you the knowledge and power to customize the software and technologies you're using to get the job done. Packt books are more specific and less general than the IT books you have seen in the past. Our unique business model allows us to bring you more focused information, giving you more of what you need to know, and less of what you don't.

Packt is a modern, yet unique publishing company, which focuses on producing quality, cutting-edge books for communities of developers, administrators, and newbies alike. For more information, please visit our website: www.packtpub.com.

Writing for Packt

We welcome all inquiries from people who are interested in authoring. Book proposals should be sent to author@packtpub.com. If your book idea is still at an early stage and you would like to discuss it first before writing a formal book proposal, contact us; one of our commissioning editors will get in touch with you.

We're not just looking for published authors; if you have strong technical skills but no writing experience, our experienced editors can help you develop a writing career, or simply get some additional reward for your expertise.

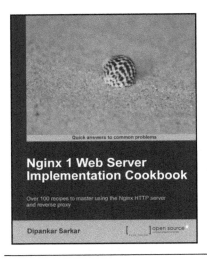

Nginx 1 Web Server Implementation Cookbook

ISBN: 978-1-849514-96-5   Paperback: 236 pages

Over 100 recipies to master using the Ngnix HTTP server and reverse proxy

1. Quick recipes and practical techniques to help you maximize your experience with Nginx

2. Interesting recipes that will help you optimize your web stack and get more out of your existing setup

3. Secure your website and prevent your setup from being compromised using SSL and rate-limiting techniques

CentOS 6 Linux Server Cookbook

ISBN: 978-1-849519-02-1   Paperback: 374 pages

A practical guide to installing, configuring, and administering the CentOS community-based enterprise server

1. Delivering comprehensive insight into CentOS server with a series of starting points that show you how to build, configure, maintain and deploy the latest edition of one of the world's most popular community based enterprise servers.

2. Providing beginners and more experienced individuals alike with the opportunity to enhance their knowledge by delivering instant access to a library of recipes that addresses all aspects of CentOS server and put you in control.

3. Giving you immediate access to a thriving knowledge base that illustrates just how quickly you can master CentOS server with a whole host of tricks of the trade thrown in for good measure.

Please check **www.PacktPub.com** for information on our titles

Linux Mint System Administrator's Beginner's Guide

ISBN: 978-1-849519-60-1   Paperback: 146 pages

A practical guide to learn basic concepts, techniques, and tools to become a Linux Mint system administrator

1. Discover Linux Mint and learn how to install it

2. Learn basic shell commands and how to deal with user accounts

3. Find out how to carry out system administrator tasks such as monitoring, backups, and network configuration

Scalix: Linux Administrator's Guide

ISBN: 978-1-847192-76-9   Paperback: 276 pages

Install, configure, and administer your Scalix Collaboration Platform email and groupware server

1. Install, upgrade, and configure Scalix

2. Build a robust and reliable system

3. Detailed walkthroughs and expert advice on best practices

Please check **www.PacktPub.com** for information on our titles

www.ingramcontent.com/pod-product-compliance
Lightning Source LLC
Chambersburg PA
CBHW060459060326
40689CB00020B/4587